Dear Nan,

Bob and you as
neighbors and friends have
meant so much to us —
I thank you for your friendship
and wish you all the best
and happiness

The cover picture of
me was at Bohemian Grove
as a guest of Bob with Jeff
and Walter attending.

Any Auto-Bio is a bit of
an ego trip — but I hope
this dispells any idea
that I am a blue blood.

Sincerely,
Hank

Virtute et opera

Harris

I Did It My Way

but with a lot of help!

Francis (Frank) Meetze Harris

KELLER PUBLISHING
Marco Island, Florida

Designed and composed at Hobblebush Books,
Brookline, New Hampshire (www.hobblebush.com)

Printed in China by Sunquest (Shanghai) Inc.

Published by

Keller Publishing
590 Fieldstone Dr.
Marco Island, FL 34145

KellerPublishing.com
800-631-1952

To Susie, my wife of 50 plus years and soul mate for life.
You never failed to believe in me
when I was often very unsure of what to do.

Acknowledgment

While "I did it my way" is the theme and title of this book—nobody does it alone.

Many people have helped me survive and succeed by offering support and criticism of my attitudes and actions.

Foremost are my mother and father who, through tough times of economic depression, World War II, personal injuries and hard work, guided me, and encouraged me, to do better. Their advice and council always rings in my head as I look back.

In the small town of Lincolnton, North Carolina there were outstanding teachers whom I acknowledge in this book. They, by word and action, served as important role models.

Contents

INTRODUCTION   xiv

LIST OF ILLUSTRATIONS   ix

1   The Harris Lineage   1

2   Early Life in Lincolnton   5

3   Small Town Characters   10

4   Dad's Gas Station and Country Store   15

5   Adversity Teaches Me Perseverance   18

6   Fast Times and the Discovery of Golf   22

7   On To College   25

8   Interview with Owens-Illinois   31

9   On the Corporate Ladder   35

10   Susie   37

11   Romance Blooms   39

12   Marriage   42

13   On Up the Ladder   52

14   Plastic Bottles at Owens-Illinois   54

15   Back to Toledo   61

16   Losing Dad and Mom   66

17   Trouble Brewing and a Way Out   68

18   On My Own and Thinking Big   72

19   Blasting Off   77

20   The Oil Embargo and the FDA Take a Bite   87

21   When the Going Gets Tough . . .   90

22   The Final Lap   93

23 Helping Others Help Themselves   104

24 Country Club Champion   106

25 Pine Valley   108

26 A New Direction   116

27 Despite the Blackmail   119

28 Dodging a Bullet   126

29 Various Boards and the IPE   128

30 YPO and a Special Friend, Gary Player   132

31 Hunting and Fishing   135

32 Golf: Good Friends, Wonderful Places   149

33 Wealth and Posterity   165

34 Our Children   169

EPILOGUE   177

APPENDIX A (Susie's Membership in NSCDA)   183

APPENDIX B (Correspondence on Dean of
    UNC-Chapel Hill)   193

APPENDIX C (Letter from Robert O. Ebert)   199

APPENDIX D (Letter from Samuel I. Carter)   201

APPENDIX E (Letter from Arthur R. McCamey, Jr.)   203

APPENDIX F (A brief history of Josh Rothman)   205

APPENDIX G (A brief history of Jennifer Harris)   207

List of Illustrations

1. High school yearbook picture   xiv
2. Most Original   xv
3. Working the Round Room at Bigwin Inn   26
4. Tending bar   27
5. Bob Wailes and my niece Jacquelyn Harris Wailes   30
6. Our wedding picture, September 29, 1956   43
7. Our wedding invitation   44
8. Newly married   45
9. Susie and her father, "Biggie" Draper   45
10. Jim Irwin, brother Jack, my best man, Frank Harris, Dad (Walter)   46
11. Bride's Maids   46
12. View from river front yard of home which was Welles, then Draper and then Harris   47
13. The big wedding reception tent with views of the river   47
14. "Let them eat cake"   48
15. With brother Jack and Malcolm Ward, the Episcopal priest   48
16. Mae Welles, Susie's grandmother, Pinkie Harris, Frank's mother, and Virginia Dogan, Frank's aunt   49
17. Susie and grandmother Welles   49
18. Susie with sister Donna   50
19. Susie with her mother, "Tookie"   50
20. Enjoying the reception under the big tent   51
21. Our house on Summer Hill Dr., Phoenix Maryland in 1960 when I became District Manager in Baltimore   56
22. Duck hunting, circa 1966. To my left are Tom Swigart and Jack Harris   58

23. Goose hunt circa 1967, Eastern Shore, Maryland   59

24. Our Perrysburg house   62

25. Paddle tennis at the Toledo Country Club   63

26. My Mom at the Waldorf Astoria on her trip to New York City   67

27. My Dad and Mom with Walter and Gingi when they came to see us in Ohio, circa 1969   67

28. With Bob Ebert on an Alaska trip   71

29. With Bill Laimbeer at the Grand Hotel, Mackinac Island, Michigan   76

30. Letter to my parents during the founding of AIM Packaging   78

31. Son Walter after a duck hunt at our lodge   80

32. Heading to the duck blind with my dog   81

33. Grouse hunting with Susie, circa 1966   82

34. With Bill Stokely, CEO of Stokely-Van Camp after a productive duck hunt   83

35. The Cessna 421 owned by AIM Packaging Company   85

36. Art & Ann McCamey, Sam & Betty Carter, Susie   86

37. The two sides of my good friend Jim White. "On the other hand!"   94

38. A wonderful party for my 70th birthday   95

39. Russ Gervais and his wife at the America's Cup Race 1984   98

40. With business partner Art McCamey   99

41. Great friends Art and Anne McCamey   99

42. Sam Carter, Frank Harris, Art McCamey   101

43. Letter from John Dorey   102

44. Note from Gerry Behm, my secretary for 20 years   103

45. Letter from Mike Brinker   105

46. My email to Sandy (Frank) Tatum   110

47. Sandy response   111

48. Another win at Pine Valley   113

49. Spinning a tall tale or joke at Pine Valley   114

50. With Jerry Dirven and Jim White   114

51. With Dan Quayle at Pine Valley   115

52. With John B. McCoy, former Chair/CEO Bank One   121

53. Green Cove Resort and Wild Wings Marine and R.V. Park   125

54. Thank you note on retiring as a board member of Brazeway   129

55. Write-up in the *Carolina Alumni Review*, Winter 1987   130
56. I resigned from the IPE in 1999   131
57. With good friends Pat and Bob Ebert   135
58. Goose hunting trip to Belcher Island, 1973   136
59. Fishing in Alaska   137
60. Miller Meyers, former head of Dairy Queen International, in Alaska, 1993   138
61. Alaska 1994   139
62. Our house at 227 Polynesia Court, Marco Island   140
63. Christmas on Marco Island in the '70s   141
64. Another good day in the Gulf of Mexico out from Naples/Marco   141
65. Another good catch   142
66. Took son Walter for a big day of tarpon fishing   142
67. On one of many visits to the King Ranch   143
68. Grouse shooting in Scotland   144
69. Our good friends Dick and Sissy King   147
70. Susie with shotgun at King's Ranch   147
71. King and Queen at Bunratty Castle Ireland   148
72. Golf swing and follow through   149
73. Becky, 1980, my first Labrador Retriever   153
74. Nessie, a good Black Lab   153
75. Hawk, the last and best   153
76. Thank you note from Gene Sarazen   154
77. One "Great Day." Beat Gordon Brewer, former U.S. Senior Amateur Champ on his course   155
78. Acceptance of my resignation from being a *Golf Digest* panelist   158
79. Playing golf in Ireland and Scotland with good friends   162
80. Dan Ferguson's personal plane (not corporate) which we took to Ireland, Scotland and England   163
81. First time to shoot my age or better, June 2000   163
82. Letter from Sam Nunn subsequent to his visit to Naples and speech to the Forum Club   164
83. Becky, Walter, Frank, Susie, Gingi   169
84. L-R Gingi, Frank, Susie, Walter   170
85. Gingi, Addy and Susie in our Maumee home   170

86. Granddaughter Addy Rothman at 16 years of age 171

87. Grandson Sam Rothman at 14 years of age   171

88. Daughter Gingi as a teacher and "Soccer Mom," 2006

89. Son Walter with a grouper on Marco Island   173

90. Walter with a pheasant in Ohio 173

91. Frank, Susie, Jennifer, Walter, Gingi, Josh, Sam and Addy   174

92. Jennifer K. Harris, son Walter's wife   175

93. Jennifer and Walter at rehearsal dinner the night before they
    married   175

94. Grandsons Grant C. Harris (5) and Welles F. Harris (7)   176

95. Family picture circa 1996   176

Introduction

I, FRANCIS MEETZE HARRIS, was born January 15, 1933, in the small North Carolina town of Lincolnton. It was a Norman Rockwell or Mayberry type of environment. We said a blessing at every meal and went to church. We were far from holier-than-thou-ers, but these were the socially acceptable things that you did in a small town in the south.

Seems like everybody knows everything that goes on in a small town, and they watch out for you, for better or worse. In a little town like Lincolnton, there were clearly defined classes of people when it came to wealth. At the top were the mill owners, bankers, other big business owners, and big land owners. Middle class consisted of the managers and merchants, which is where my parents fit in. And then there were the workers in the mills and the furniture factories.

Yellow buses brought kids in from the farms five to 15 miles out in the red dirt country of North Carolina. Probably 70 percent of my high school classmates were from the boonies and rode in on those yellow busses. If you lived within a couple of miles from school, you walked. There was very little class distinction in terms of who your friends were, unless you were just poor white trash. You played with your friends; you sang with them, you dated them. They were your community.

My family was not poor as I was growing up. We had a nice house, a nice piece of ground, and dad had a business. We had a car, a pony, and nice clothes. Even so, I was sure as hell hungry to live like the wealthy people did and have the freedom they enjoyed. I was later to translate that hunger into a successful college and business career.

My hunger and ambition developed from a competitive standpoint. I always liked to be the best, the fastest, throw the ball the farthest, catch the ball with one hand, make a diving leap to catch a baseball, catch the biggest fish—all trying to get respect through recognition of achievements. That competitive ambition has served me well in this life.

The envy I once had of kids from wealthy families is now in most cases sympathy for their lack of drive. It's very hard to make someone hungry when he has been stuffed all his life.

It seems, as I look back, that many of the best students and athletes "peak" too soon and rest on their laurels, never achieving their potential.

Insecurity with a large dose of vanity, in my case, was a double-edged sword, which sometimes produced praise and sometimes resentment. The caption under my high school year book photo (below) was perhaps more prophetic that anyone realized at the time. Being original, different and singular was recognized, but not always loved. I was however voted most original boy in the list of Senior Superlatives.

FRANK M. HARRIS
"FROSS"
"A self-made man who worships his creator."
Band; Glee Club; Wolf Staff; PINE BURR Staff; French Club; "Lady of the Terrace"; "Spooks and Spasms"; Class Lawyer; English Club.

HIGH SCHOOL YEARBOOK PICTURE

MOST ORIGINAL

And of course I have to give thanks to old blue eyes, the Chairman of the Board, Frank Sinatra, for the inspiration for the title to this memoir. I've long identified with the following lyrics, made famous by Sinatra (see next page).

My Way

And now, the end is here
And so I face the final curtain.
My friend, I'll say it clear
I'll state my case, of which I'm certain.
I've lived a life that's full.
I traveled each and ev'ry highway.
And more, much more than this, I did it my way.
Regrets, I've had a few
But then again, too few to mention.
I did what I had to do and saw it through without exemption.
I planned each charted course, each careful step along the byway.
And more, much more than this, I did it my way.
Yes, there were times, I'm sure you knew
When I bit off more than I could chew.
But through it all, when there was doubt
I ate it up and spit it out
I faced it all and I stood tall and did it my way.
I've loved, I've laughed and cried.
I've had my fill, my share of losing.
And now, as tears subside, I find it all so amusing.
To think I did all that
And may I say, not in a shy way,
"Oh, no, oh, no, not me, I did it my way"
For what is a man, what has he got?
If not himself, then he has naught
To say the things he truly feels and not the words of one who kneels
The record shows I took the blows and did it my way!

1

The Harris Lineage

Both my parents—Pinkie Marbelle Meetze Harris and Walter Lee Harris—had nine siblings. Consequently I've been blessed with many aunts and uncles as well as a multitude of first cousins. I was well acquainted with this extended family during my early childhood as family visits were about all my family did for holidays. They did not have the time or money for vacations or to travel very far. This large caring bunch of relatives provided much joy for all of us when we got together.

On my father's side the Harris-Barringer clan of ancestors go way back to the early 1700s with some very successful and notable members who arrived in Pennsylvania and migrated south as land owners, medical doctors, revolutionary and civil war soldiers. Grandfather Walter Lonie Harris grew up in China Grove, Rowan County, North Carolina where he was a county commissioner and well respected. He lived in a great big house of no particular architectural magnificence. However it was heated by wood burning fireplaces in practically every room, quite respectable for that time but barely adequate for the winter cold of North Carolina. The house had indoor plumbing and other features. (There were some family furniture heirlooms that, unfortunately, later went to my brother, Jack, because he was the oldest and to other members of the family.)

On my mother's side, the Meetze-Frank group were later arrivals to America. They were German Hessians, hired by the British to help put down the American Revolution. After landing at Charleston, South Carolina circa 1775 and, being so badly treated by the British, they deserted to join the fledgling American army. Joining up with the famous "Swamp Fox," General Francis Marion, they fought and prevailed over the British in what is now South Carolina and Georgia. In honor of the Swamp Fox the name Francis was bestowed on generations of Meetze men all the way down to Francis (Frank) Harris.

My wife's ancestors go even further back to the very early settlers of America. Susie is a proud, registered member of The National Society of the Colonial Dames of America, which was founded in 1891 in Philadelphia to promote interest in colonial history. Eligibility is determined by descent from certain categories of civil servants in the colonies who served on or before 6 July 1776. The NSCDA provides scholarships, publishes books, and preserves paintings, manuscripts, and buildings of historic importance. In 2001, the organization had fifteen thousand members. Susie's membership is by descent from William Leete who resided in Hartford, Connecticut until his death April 16, 1683. (For a complete tracing of this ancestry see Appendix A.)

All of Susie's ancestors were Yankees who settled in Massachusetts, Connecticut, New York and later in Ohio, Missouri, Illinois and Iowa. One of her ancestors was John Hunt whose memoirs we had published. He was one of the first settlers in the Toledo/Maumee area with a trading post along the river. A leading civic leader, he represented the area before statehood with trips to Washington and other parts of the emerging nation. It's reported that he witnessed the return of Lewis and Clark to St. Louis after their journey of exploration to the Pacific Ocean.

Susie's great grandfather, George D. Welles, was a general in the Union Army. At the end of the War Between the States my great grandfather Meetze, a major in the Confederate Army, had the rather unpleasant duty of surrendering to General Welles near Durham, North Carolina. Susie's lineage includes many very successful Welles and Drapers, both financially and in civic stature, as lawyers, investors and executives. One distant Welles relative is presently a billionaire having made his fortune from scratch, starting a small company and building it into a big one.

It would take another complete book to write all that is known about our ancestors on both sides of the family. So, for now, I will only say it is a proud heritage that I enjoy.

I have tried to stay in touch with Sarah Hough, my last living aunt on my mother's side, and with cousins on both the Meetze and Harris sides. Still living cousins on the Meetze side include Kathrine Mann Todd (David), Jim and John Pridgen, David Simpson, Sally Hough Blackwelder (John), Jim Hough, Donald and Gene Brantly, Ellen Betty and Tootsy Hudson. On the Harris side there are Charlie Henderson, Lucy Henderson Robinson, Nancy Cattarius, Lonnie Harris, Mary Jo Holland. Susie stays in touch with Jim Draper, Ben Dansard and some of his children.

It's getting pretty thinned out now as father time takes its toll. The 2nd and 3rd cousins have little interest in old family stuff it seems.

Before closing out this chapter I should relate what I know of my parents early life.

My mother, Pinkie Marbelle Meetze Harris, descended from the Hessian mercenaries who became American patriots, was one of 10 children—seven girls and three boys—in a farm family near Salisbury, North Carolina. Fourth in the line of her sisters she was a very attractive young woman who remained very attractive through her 70s, posing many times as a model. She grew up in a very close-knit family with a wonderful father and a rather autocratic mother, on a hundred-acre farm near Salisbury. I never knew my grandmother very well as she died when I was quite young. Her last name was Frank. I recall my grandfather Meetze as a gentle, pleasant man, who was very wiry and strong.

Mom's early childhood, I suspect, was pretty simple, filled with all the farm activities from helping to plant crops to helping reap them. They must have had a big garden to feed a family of that size. She attended Catawba College in Salisbury for one year and was married at about age 20 to my father, Walter Lee Harris, who was about 30 years old at the time.

My father, like my mother, grew up in a family of 10 children in China Grove, North Carolina.

Grandfather Harris could not afford to send them all to college. He sent the six girls to college and sent the boys to work very early in life, since their farm was not able to support everyone. Father was next to oldest of the 10 children.

After my parents' marriage in 1925, they moved to Detroit, where my father worked for the Ford Motor Company and Mother worked for the J. L. Hudson Department Store. Dad rose from production worker to foreman. The young couple lived at Palmer Park, which is now a black ghetto, but it was a pretty nice little area at that time. They were doing reasonably well when my brother, Jack Rondal Harris, was born in 1928. Two of my father's brothers, Earl and Bill, were also in Detroit with their families, so they stayed in touch. My parents had quite a few friends in Detroit. As a very young man, I had the opportunity to meet many of them when we visited.

At that time, I'm sure it was quite an experience for my parents to be in Detroit in a burgeoning economic environment, after growing up in an agrarian family in China Grove and Salisbury.

Everything went along well for them until the Depression hit after the stock market crash of 1929. The auto industry was severely crippled and my parents returned to Lincolnton, North Carolina.

2

Early Life in Lincolnton

Right after my parents returned to North Carolina from Detroit, my father found a job through a relative, Warren Mann, head of the state's road building and maintenance department. My father became a manager of road maintenance in two counties of North Carolina—Lincoln and Cabarrus counties. At the department, he was known as Captain Harris, or Cap Harris—a name that stuck with him from then on. He worked there for several years before and after I was born. My parents rented the McAlaster house, and my father's work was mostly a happy experience. Father got along well with many of the more prominent people in our town. They liked his sense of humor, and he was quite popular.

I recall my father was an extremely strong, aggressive person with a big voice, big, strong shoulders, and the strongest handshake one could imagine. He wore very thick glasses because of his poor eyesight and had almost albino-light skin with a blonde, balding head. He was quite quick and bright even though he had only an eighth-grade education. Dad was a very tough taskmaster who had little tact. It was always, "Hey, boy, go do this," and, "Hey, boy, go do that." That's the way he was raised. He learned to speak that way to his underlings in the Detroit factories. Also, that's the way he talked to the prisoners on the chain gangs with his road department job. He was very demanding of my brother and me. We didn't love it, but we survived. Father was not particularly lovable most of the time. He had a lot of aches and pains from an accident. He would come home tired from work and we had dinner quietly. He was not the most pleasant person to be around because he was so critical. You answered him, "Yes, sir/No, sir," and you talked back at your peril.

Conversely, mother was sweet and kind. She sewed, cooked dinner, raked leaves, planted the garden and generally took care of home maintenance. Special interests were flowers, decorating, and antiques. She loved to travel rural roads and find people who had old pieces of furniture. She'd buy their furniture from them and refinish it with our help. She especially loved furniture made of walnut and pine, and Civil War antiques from wealthy family estates. She collected a lot of glassware and oil lamps, which we eventually electrified. She amassed such a large collection that she started an antique store in our home. It wasn't particularly successful.

One early December day in 1935, my father had taken my mother to a beauty parlor. On the way home, a drunk driver broadsided his car. He lay unconscious for over 30 days and nearly died. He survived but was partially paralyzed for the rest of his life with slurred speech and a limp that he was somewhat able to correct over time. It was an extremely difficult time. I was 2 when it happened. Many of my aunts and uncles came to help around the house. My earliest memories were of my dad lying there almost in a coma. When he came out of it, he was unable to work for the road department.

Having come from farm families, mother and dad raised all the necessities for food that they could. Our garden was a big source of our food supply, especially during World War II. We also raised pigs, chickens and a cow. Hogs were slaughtered every fall, and in spring we planted a big garden. My brother Jack and I worked in the garden, raked leaves, and mucked out the stable for our pony, Silver. We did everything from pitching hay to shoveling manure.

In 1939 we moved into a new house that my father had built for $10,000—a lot of money in those days. The property was six partially wooded acres on S. Aspen Street on the edge of town. It included a creek that I could follow for miles without seeing another house. That's where I learned to love hunting and fishing and just being out in the wild. The house was two stories with only the lower story finished. The upstairs bedrooms where Jack and I slept had unfinished rafters and studs. The only bathroom was downstairs. We had "central heat," which meant there was a little hall in the middle of the house from which all the doors opened; we closed doors to distribute the heat. Even though heat rises, it was very cold upstairs for Jack and me. The house was heated by coal, which was shoveled by hand. We put in oil heat after World War II. The radio was the only entertainment in the house. The family sat around in a small, smoke-filled room listening to Jack Benny, Amos and Andy, Lum and Abner, and the news of the war.

I grew up with kids whose fathers were active hunters and fishermen, so we all were too. My father wasn't able to hunt because of his poor eyesight, but he always had a shotgun. Everybody had a gun. We'd shoot rabbits, quail, and squirrels—just about whatever jumped up.

The creek provided sunfish and catfish that we caught on a stick with a string, bobber, and hook with a worm or caterpillar for bait. I remember the thrill of pulling a fish bigger than an adult's hand out of the water—maybe 10 inches long. In some places, the water was pretty shallow. We seined with gunny sacks that we cut open and nailed to sticks. We then moved back under the bank and caught whatever popped in there and had all kinds of fun doing that. We sometimes dammed narrow parts of the stream that were about 20 to 25 feet wide with gunnysacks filled with sand and created our own swimming hole. We had a tree with a rope hanging on it, and we would swing out over the dam and drop into the swimming hole.

One of the kids I grew up with was Johnny Shuford. His family was quite prominent in the area. His cousins owned the textile mills and his father, Ox Shuford, had been an outstanding athlete at the University of North Carolina. Ox was a huge man who played on the football team and boxed. I guess he had his bell rung a few too many times because he had a difficult time talking. But he was a colorful guy liked by everyone. He was still quite famous from his outstanding performance on the football team at the University of North Carolina.

We lived about five doors down from the Shufords. I'll never forget December 7, 1941. I was eight years old. It was a bright, cold Sunday morning. After returning from church, I was walking down to the creek looking at some frozen patches along the edge of the stream. Johnny came up to me and told me about the Japanese attack on Pearl Harbor. I didn't have much emotion when I heard it because I didn't know what he was talking about. It only galvanized in my mind later when I saw pictures on the newsreels of the terrible explosions of the attack. At the time Johnny told me about it, I had no concept of what Pearl Harbor was or where it was.

The farm environment we grew up in enabled us to get Silver, our pony. He was a white, five-gaited horse with a black head and tail. We got him when I was four as my dad always thought we needed a pony and I agreed. It was terrific for me to be able to ride Silver most of the time without a saddle. I'd just jump on his back and go visit my friends or wherever I wanted. I'd just drop the bridle over on the ground and let the horse graze while I was playing baseball or football. We tried to show the pony with a saddle on him but he wasn't that good, and I wasn't that good in horse shows. But we had a good time trying.

We also had a dog named Snow King, a spitz blend with thick white hair. He was a big, mean dog that slept under the back porch in a box lined with a gunny sack. We didn't have any inside dogs. We did have some cats that stayed in the barn with the horses and caught rats.

My first gun was a single shot .22 rifle. It probably cost $20. I was often successful picking off a squirrel or a rabbit but it wasn't particularly sporting of me, however, because I had to get them while they were sitting still. We did a lot of target practice on coffee can lids. As I got older, I was able to use my dad's Ithaca 12-gauge shotgun. It was lethal. I could walk around our acreage and sometimes come back with four rabbits.

I was quite a good shot at an early age. One day, I was hunting rabbits by the creek while one of my friends watched me from the highway bridge that went over the creek. I shot two rabbits just while he was watching. Impressed, he said, "Golly, Frank, that was really something. Good shooting."

3

Small Town Characters

Every small town is full of interesting characters. Each person I knew affected me in some way, some more positively than others. But it was in the small town of Lincolnton that I learned to deal with every type of character—something that assisted me in my successful rise as an executive and entrepreneur. I once observed that many CEOs of major corporations come from small towns. They knew how to get along with other people of all levels. They knew how to have respect, and they didn't look down on others.

I had a neighbor named Harry Hoyle. Sometimes we were friends, and sometimes we'd fight. His father was the local Ford dealer. They lived in a very imposing home on a hill near us. We played all the sports together, and he was a pretty good athlete. Harry was a year older than I was, and it seemed to make a lot of difference. He was a good looking kid who eventually married my first sweetheart, a majorette whose name was Ibby—short for Elizabeth—Abernathy. She was the daughter of, supposedly, the wealthiest people in town. (Harry's and Ibby's marriage was a blessing for me because she became extremely corpulent as she got older.) When I was in the high school band, I switched from playing trumpet to trombone to get closer to where she was doing her majorette dancing. She was extremely well endowed, bust-wise, for a high school girl.

As kids, we used to fight to settle disputes—just quick little fights that lasted two minutes with a lot of bluffing around and taking a few cuts. Once in a while, somebody got hit in the nose or the eye, but nobody got really hurt. Where I grew up, if you were offended, you smacked somebody. This was done to me and by me. It was more our pride than our bodies that got hurt when we were beaten. Of course the other kids were egging us on if they were around when we were all playing football or baseball and anyone got in a fight. I had a little more temper than strength, so I sometimes got into some fights and came out less than a winner. I did that until I got into high school and got involved with a kid named Jim Boss who was a Golden Gloves boxer. He beat me up pretty badly, and my mother told me, "Son, if you're looking for a fight, you can find one on every corner. I recommend that you think twice before you get that involved."

Jim Stamey's family owned a little two-pump gas station near where we lived. He was a little smaller than I was, and I beat up on him a little bit. One day, his older brother came and smacked me so hard I saw stars. I figured I'd better not try to be the best fighter because someone else always had a friend or family member who could whip me.

Back in those days, we had sandlot baseball and football, and we'd all choose up teams. We played tackle football later on when we got bigger. We had a great time passing and punting. We also played basketball in Bill Elliott's backyard using a hoop made out of an old barrel stay nailed to a couple of boards, and some kind of ball that wasn't an official basketball. Bill was the son of a very prominent doctor. Mrs. Abernathy—Ibby's aunt—eventually gave us an official basketball hoop and backboard. We put it up in a little field behind Bill Elliott's house and were able to get a man with a mule and drag pan to come in there and level it off to create a dirt basketball court with only one basket and backboard.

Bill Elliott was rather pudgy and not very athletic. He became a doctor and had a very good practice in Indianapolis. Unfortunately, he came down with a horrible disease, which I think has taken his life by now. He was a well-known doctor in that area and very involved with the opera and symphony

Gordon Crowell was the son of Dr. Lester Crowell, the doctor who attended to me when I was so badly injured by burns. Gordon became a doctor as well. The family had the Crowell Hospital, a 30 or 40- room hospital in Lincolnton across the street from where the family lived.

Jack Caskey had a brother who pitched in minor league professional ball, and Jack himself was probably the finest natural athlete I can remember in baseball or football. He was a good looking kid—one of those people who stands out. Joel Connor was another outstanding athlete in football and baseball—both in grammar school and later in high school.

Johnny Lowder, the son of the superintendent of schools, was an outstanding basketball player who also won the club championship at golf at the Lincolnton Country Club. He seemed to have everything going for him. After being valedictorian he went on to the University of North Carolina. He was in medical school when he killed himself.

Johnny's father, S. Ray Lowder, was both a great scolder of my behavior and a mentor. He was a very strong, corpulent guy with enormous energy. He sometimes substituted as the band director while I was in the high school band, and he could play a trumpet better than anyone. He played John Philip Sousa marches with great enthusiasm, and we loved it. A good friend of my parents, Mr. Lowder made a great difference in my life, telling me to "straighten up" and "fly right." I drank too much beer in high school, drove too fast, and had a few too many fights. Mr. Lowder was always an inspiration to do something better.

Tommy Harkey was the son of a preacher. As somebody once suggested, the children of preachers are often the wildest. Tommy certainly lived up to that theory. He was a good baseball and football player. We frequently walked the creek and went fishing together. We were pals.

I went to church fairly regularly and was scolded by the preacher if I didn't show up. In a little town, they noticed when there was one missing from the flock of 50 to 60 in the Lutheran Church. I knew all the hymns and sang in the choir. My father's family was Episcopalian, and my mother's was Lutheran. I was very active in Sunday school and went to summer Bible school camp. Mrs. Beam, the Sunday school teacher, always tried to persuade me to become a preacher. She was relentless.

"You would just make a wonderful preacher," she said. I was 10 to 12 years old then, and I was trying to be like my brother, who was driving cars, drinking beer, and dating girls. I didn't have a proclivity to being a preacher. I didn't do anything terrible, but I was certainly marginal.

Charles Ramseur was one of my history teachers. He was a little skinny guy from a nice family who lived very near my dad's service station across from the high school. He had a marvelous singing voice. He was very helpful as I was coming along. I even got a wonderful letter from him after he saw a newspaper review of a speech I made in Charlotte. In the letter he said he thought I was a cut above everyone else in his class. That was 30 years after high school. It was nice to be remembered.

My English teacher, Mrs. Ramseuer, was about 4´ 11˝ tall. A terribly unattractive woman, she was known as "Snarl Ramseuer" because she had an almost disfigured mouth. But she was superb as an English teacher. In her class she was tough. If we didn't express ourselves and write well we had to do extra work. I made high grades in English under Snarl, both written and spoken. She was a great teacher. My wife was a language major at Vassar, and will from time to time comment when I use poor English, "Snarl would not approve of that" (which, of course, means she doesn't approve either).

Mrs. Smith was my math teacher. She was an inspiration, which I needed, not being very good in math. I didn't do my homework adequately. I didn't make very good grades, but she pushed me to do better.

My geometry teacher, Mrs. Ferguson, was important to my ego. I was good at geometry as visualization was something I could do very well. I'm a half-assed architect in construction projects, whether it's condos or remodeling a house. I once wrote a poem when I was in geometry class. It was in iambic pentameter like Joyce Kilmer's "Trees," and it went, "I hope I'll never see a subject as strange as geometry, with parallel boards beneath my feet, and rectangles on my desk and seat." The rest of it was published in the high school paper. It's one of the little memories that make looking back so pleasant.

Ernie Boger owned a textile mill in Boger City, a little village suburb of Lincolnton that had been named after him. (He eventually sold out to Burlington.) He was from Philadelphia and was a rather attractive man with a lot of money and a fancy home. He had a Lincoln Continental convertible back in the days when they had a spare tire on the back. He was very helpful to me when I was going through the agonies of adolescence, by giving me a little book by Mary Baker Eddy, the founder of the Christian Science movement. I began using the prayer in there daily. It read, "The Lord is with me. The Lord is helping me. The Lord is guiding me. And if God is for me, who can be against me?" It's a standard prayer that I continue to use every day. I'm not a Christian Scientist, and I didn't even know what they were when he gave me that book. That book and Norman Vincent Peale's *The Power of Positive Thinking* were very important to me as I was growing up.

Ernie Boger was a great guy to talk to about a kid's ambitions. He asked me once, "What do you want to do for a living when you grow up?" I didn't know for sure, but I said, "I'd like to be an executive." He laughed and said, "Well, who doesn't?" When I got into college and made the dean's list, he gave me a very nice present—a cigarette lighter. It was back in the days when everybody smoked. Mr. Boger was a guiding light when it came to my ambition. He had a lot of money and a lot of things—the trappings of wealth, a lovely home, and other things that I thought someday I'd like to have.

I haven't seen my childhood buddies for 60-plus years, but I keep these great memories of all the good times we had. And I'll never forget the lessons I learned from these small town people.

4

Dad's Gas Station and Country Store

Eventually, after his terrible accident, my father was able to rent a two-pump service station in Lincolnton. It served as a country store as well, selling everything from snuff, chewing tobacco, and cigarettes to candy, soft drinks, and ice cream. Dad wasn't able to do strenuous things at the station, because of his injuries. Primarily, he sat behind the counter and rang up sales. The big chores of a service station—pumping gas, checking oil, wiping windshields, greasing and oil-changing cars, and washing them—were left to Jack and me or hired help.

One day, when I'd been working at the service station with my dad, we had some kind of argument. I went home crying. I got his shotgun and headed off into the woods. Suddenly, two quail jumped up. I shot one quail in the air and missed the second one. I'll never forget finding that beautiful feathered quail, bringing it home, and mother cooking it for me. And then my stern and critical dad came home and asked, "Did you shoot him on the ground?" I almost started crying again. He said, "You can't hit quail in the air!" I was 11 or 12 then. That shotgun was huge, but I always had great hand-eye coordination in every sport that I took part in.

With his health situation after the accident, my dad would come home every afternoon and take a nap for an hour or two to try to recover. Mother would go down and take care of the service station while he slept. The service station was open from 7 a.m. to 7 p.m. six days a week and on Sundays after church from 1 p.m. to 6 p.m. The days were long, but happily, there was an up side to it. People would come in for gas, oil, Cokes, and smokes, and dad's place became a social center of that little section of town.

I had a wonderful hunting experience with an old man named Mr. Henry, who owned a Western Auto store in town. I had just received boots and hunting clothes for Christmas. He came by my dad's service station as he was preparing to go deer hunting in Brevard in the mountains of North Carolina.

He said to me, "Son, you look like somebody who would like to go hunting."

"Yes, sir, I sure would."

"Well, why don't you just get in the car and go with us?"

Mom and Dad were just opening up the store. I asked, "Can I go? Can I go?"

Dad said, "Mr. Henry, you sure you want to take him?"

"Yeah, we'd be glad to have him."

So I got in the car. I didn't have a change of clothes or anything. We drove about three or four hours up into the mountain. I was sitting in the back seat with two whiskey-drinking men. By the time we got to the mountain with Mr. Henry driving, they were drunk. We stayed at a rustic hunting lodge. My first hunting experience there was a flop. It rained most of the time, and we just sat on the porch. We never did see a deer, but when it cleared up, I carried a big bolt action rifle for Mr. Henry as we went into the woods. He had a shotgun too. What an experience watching these guys play poker and sit and talk. Some of them were great talkers, great yarn tellers, and joke tellers—something that would later help me develop quite a knack for storytelling.

Dr. Lester Crowell, a well-respected doctor in town, walked on crutches and had braces on his legs, which were limp following infantile paralysis, or polio. His car was equipped with the gear, accelerator, and brake controls mounted in the steering wheel. He had the most marvelous personality—articulate, funny, and smart. I'll never forget when he drove up to my dad's service station one day, and I rushed out to see what I could do for him. He said, "I don't need any gas this time, Harris, but bring me a female Hershey bar."

I did.

He said, "That's great. You understood. No nuts."

As I grew up in my dad's service station, I listened to his cronies tell jokes and stories. That's also how I became good at telling stories myself. During my time later in life as a salesman, I used those stories while doing business and during leisure activities. I'm at the point where I can probably go on a month's trip with people and tell 10 stories a day without repeating myself. They're stories that range from mildly humorous to hilariously absurd. I'm routinely called on to tell stories at Pine Valley Golf Club in New Jersey, where storytelling is the dessert of the evening. I have often been called upon to be the clean-up man, so to speak, batting last. I never forget a good story.

If you tell stories, people will tell you more. I get 10 a day on the Internet alone. People are always calling me on the phone saying, "Frank, have you heard this one?" I've become so good that if you give me a category and a few seconds, I can tell you a humorous story that will tie in to it. Sandy Tatum, the former head of the U.S. Golf Association, had to make a speech in San Francisco. He e-mailed me to give him some material to entertain the people. He's a pretty straight arrow otherwise. He said, "My wife has told me to lighten up, put some humor in it." So I sent him some material.

I was never a particularly good student unless I had to be. I was never outstanding in musical talent. I really relied on personality all my life, which enabled me to become a damn good salesman. I was able, and still am, to read other people and define their hot buttons. I've watched speakers who just keep talking even after they've lost their audience. They're rather pathetic because the other people are stone bored and these guys just keep rattling on. You have to read your audience, find out what they're interested in, and wind it down as quickly as you can. Telling great stories is my trademark, and it all started in my father's gas station.

5

Adversity Teaches Me Perseverance

I learned how to tell stories at my dad's station, but I also learned a very important life lesson while working there.

There is an axiom in this life that when you experience adversity, either you gain strength or you fail terribly. An early accident in my life gave me a depth of perseverance to keep going when things got hard. It was a lesson that helped me all along the way.

On Friday October 13, 1944, when I was 11 years old, my father went to see his dying father in Salisbury/China Grove area. I was taken out of school to help my mother at the service station, which was in the same block as the grammar school. I was only in the sixth grade, but I had already learned how to pump gas, change oil, and help with the responsibilities that accompanied being a part of the station.

That day I began to fill a customer's 1935 Ford with gasoline. It was one of the old gas tanks where, if you pumped it too fast, it would shoot back on you. I was pumping it too fast, and the gas shot out all over my corduroy pants. As I jumped back, I spilled more gas on the cement around the gas pump.

After the customer paid his bill and left, I sat out on the bench in front of the station with gas all over my pants. There in front of me was an old unlit kitchen match that somebody had dropped after trying to use it to light his pipe. Not thinking, I reached down and struck it on the concrete between my legs. I immediately exploded with gasoline flames all over my pants. My legs were baking inside.

I jumped up and ran a few feet like a kid might do in total panic. At that moment, my brother, who was in high school, and a friend of his were walking to the service station. They wrapped a coat around my legs and put the fire out.

My brother, who was impatient with me as usual, said, "Get up, Frank. You're okay."

I was in shock and someone said, "Oh no, he's badly hurt."

A friend with a car took me to the hospital, just a few blocks away. They cut my pants off. There was practically no pain at that stage. They began to peel off layer after layer of skin. Then they wrapped my legs up with some kind of grease. I went home with my legs bandaged almost to my crotch.

The pain was awful. My Aunt Beulah came to help with the situation. My grandfather had just died. Imagine—they had to go through that, and then I was home with my legs burned. My Aunt Beulah said my wolf howls from the pain were really something. I was in terrible, terrible pain.

It went on for a long time, and then an infection set in, which was almost automatic when a large area was damaged. They brought me back to the hospital, where I stayed for almost two months.

I was so badly infected that I couldn't eat or keep anything in my stomach. My weight went down to absolute skin and bones. They put my legs under an incubator with light bulbs and came in six times a day to pour potassium permanganate—a grape-colored product—on them. I don't think it did a damn bit of good, but that's probably all they knew how to do.

I listened to the doctor speak to my mother in the hall outside my door: The doctor said, "If he doesn't eat, he's not going to survive." I must say, I was pretty impressed with that declaration.

I retched with anything I ate, except Coca-Cola. I was living on sugar water.

I later heard that one of the mill owners, a nice, corpulent, balding man, asked how I was doing. My mother or father said, "He's in pretty bad shape."

"I always liked that boy," he said to them. Then he said that penicillin was available to the public for the first time apart from military use. Through his auspices, they were able to get some penicillin, which knocked down my raging infection.

In a few weeks, I was able to go home and spend my time waiting for my legs to heal. They didn't heal for almost one year. There were third degree burns below my knees and above my ankles. They were so bad I wore bandages on them for all that time.

I got to be pretty good in a wheel chair in our little house. Then I got to be pretty good on crutches. I was so determined to overcome my injuries that I actually played baseball on crutches.

This was during World War II, and it was a tough time for me to see the terribly mutilated people who were coming back from the fronts. It was also the same time of the polio outbreak in North Carolina. The hospitals were filled with kids who were in a hell of a lot worse shape than I was.

Over the next three or four years, my legs were pretty badly disfigured. They were bright red where the scar tissue had been. My red scars stung as blood vessels and nerves recovered. As time passed, my red legs became paler, but to this day still have no pigment in one eight-inch area on each leg.

I had a real spurt of growth after that. I did miss a year of school and had to go through seventh grade again, but I was able to skip the eighth grade by moving me from the seventh to the ninth grade. It wasn't because I was so brilliant; it was because, for whatever reason, they were making promotions like this.

My accident was just one of those terrible things that happened. I learned to live with these things like anybody else does, whether in a wheelchair or on crutches. I just had to get through it. People recover. I recovered and was able to be a very fast runner. I wouldn't let it hold me down. I was fast and played tackle football, using shields over the areas that I had to protect. All my life, if I ever banged my shin, it wasn't something that took a week to heal; it took a month or more. There is not enough blood in there to heal it quicker.

It turned out to be a salutary thing in a way. As I got into my senior year in high school, the Korean War was raging and so many of my friends were drafted to go to Korea. Two or three of them never came back. The draft board rated me as 4-f because of the burns. Consequently I was not eligible for military service.

Even now in my 70s it is still very evident where I got burned so I keep my legs covered most of the time with long socks. Whenever someone sees me on the beach or around a swimming pool without my socks and shoes they say, "My God, have you been walking through a flour bin? Your feet are so white."

But, you learn to live with that. I had enough aggressiveness to overcome my accident. I never let it get me down.

6

Fast Times and the Discovery of Golf

During my high school days, I was a wild, pushy, smart-ass kid who wore zoot suits and pegged pants and sported long, over-the-ears hair called a duck butt.

I often played it cool, twirling my key chain, standing out front of drug stores with my collar up. I learned to drive early and often stole the family car to go on joy rides. I smoked and drank beer with the best of them. I was definitely big into chasing girls, constantly going on dates to drive-ins, burger joints, and movies. I dated Doris Ann Lineberger, Libby Huggins, Mary Ramseur, and Mary Ann Gray—to name a few. I once borrowed a Cadillac limo for a date. I played trombone in the marching band and sang tenor in the glee club. I also played the lead in class plays and operettas.

All through my summers, I had some pretty interesting jobs: I was a soda jerk at Rexall Drug Store, and a salesman at the Firestone store, as well as assembling bicycles and lawn mowers there. I used to park cars during baseball games that were held across the street from my father's service station. I even worked at a textile mill setting up machinery. I did anything to make a buck. Of course, I filled in at my dad's service station gaining proficiency at fixing tires and simple car repairs.

The wonderful world of golf began for me when I was 15. For a summer job, I was invited to be a lifeguard at the little nine-hole country club in Lincolnton. I was delighted to do so because I had some high school girlfriends who frequented the place.

A lot of the time, there was no one on the golf course during the day. The pro, Bruce Mashburn, also worked as a greens superintendent, and his wife ran the golf shop. Mashburn (a wonderful Scottish name) and his father had been brought over to Pinehurst by Donald Ross, the famous golf course architect. We became pretty good friends. He was an even better friend of my brother because Jack was older and used to carouse with him.

When no one was on the golf course, we had a lot of time to practice our putting, blasting out of sand traps, and chipping—all the shots. We had black caddies whom we paid 50 cents or a dollar for nine holes. I spent an awful lot of time that summer with Bruce Mashburn, particularly when it wasn't good swimming weather and nobody was at the pool. He taught me the basics of the swing. We would often play four holes on a pop circuit around as it was called.

The club champion, R. G. Carter, had been champion several times and was a World War II veteran. He loved the game and would compete in Linville, Carmel, and other good courses around North Carolina. He helped me improve my swing and my discipline. I remember those lessons so well. I got a chance to play with him quite a few times which was a great honor for a rookie golfer. The first year I learned the game I was occasionally able to score in the 80s.

After my brother left for the Army, and before I went to college, my parents needed to augment the family income. We turned the barn into a rental guest house with three rooms and three baths. We also converted another separate garage into a rental with a room and a bathroom. My mom and dad started a little home motel called Ivy and Oaks and eventually rented out other rooms that had been added onto the original house. By that time, the house had been totally finished upstairs and down, and we added a room for my Grandmother Harris. She didn't stay very long, blessedly. She moved to Lakeland, Florida to live with my Aunt Virginia. None of us found her very friendly.

My parents derived an income from those rental sites, and my mother, to a large extent, did whatever cleaning and management was necessary. It helped pay for my college and their livelihood. This was fortunate because newer service stations came into being after World War II, and younger men were able to do a better job providing the services that my dad's little service station couldn't. Besides, he was getting too old for the long hours.

7

On To College

I n 1951 I entered the University of North Carolina where my brother, Jack, was already in his junior year. He was married to Mary Sasser, a research lab technician from Whiteville, whom he had met at Appalachian State Teacher's College. They had a small apartment in Victory Village, which was veteran housing. At first I moved in with them to save money. It soon proved to be too crowded, so after one semester I moved into Stacy Dorm. As a sophomore I pledged Phi Kappa Sigma, eventually becoming their social chairman.

Golf in North Carolina has always been very popular. At that time, I believe there were more golf courses there than any other state in the country. Several very good golfers, including Bill Thornton and Jim Feree, were at the University of North Carolina when I was there. Feree was a member of Sigma Chi who, after college, played on a regular tour for many years and also the senior tour. Harvey Ward was one of the most famous golfers from UNC.

Phi Kappa Sigma fraternity had several members of the university golf team who, once in a while, would ask me to round out a foursome. I was never good enough to be on the golf team. These kids came from backgrounds where they grew up in country clubs and played with all kinds of sophisticated instructors. But it was certainly a great opportunity to learn the finer points of golf and how shots could be made— not just how far you hit it but how straight and how to curve it left and right. I played as much as time would allow but my studies always got in the way. I was a distinctive C student because I thought that was adequate to get me through the University of North Carolina. I worked afternoons and never was a very good scholar.

I worked every summer "vacation" while in college. After my freshman year my roommate, Tommy Thomas, and I went to Virginia Beach where I worked at the now torn down hotel, The Pinewood, as a bell hop. It had three stories and no elevator. So I lugged bags up and down stairs for tips and a very small salary of about $25 per week. But it included food. The hotel was right on the beach so during my off hours I enjoyed beach activities with a different girl every week. Virginia Beach was very popular at that time and tourists were coming in from all over the north.

Between my sophomore and junior years, summer of '53, I got a job along with Tom Thomas and several other UNC friends at Big

I WORKED THE ROUND ROOM AT BIGWIN INN. TO MY RIGHT
ARE HUGH CROXTON OF SPARTANBURG, SC, LATER AN MD, TOM
THOMAS, ATLANTA, MY ROOMMATE AT UNC, AND ERWIN POTTS
WHO WOULD BECOME CHAIRMAN OF A NEWSPAPER CHAIN

TENDING BAR

Win Inn, a vast hotel resort on an island in the Lake of Bays, Muskoka, Ontario Canada, which is about 150 miles north of Toronto. This was a very special experience. There were about 150 of us college kids, mostly from Canada but about 20 from the U.S. And the distribution of girls versus boys was just wonderful—at least two girls for each boy. The girls worked as maids, waitresses, etc., and the boys as bar waiters, bartenders, dishwashers, boat pursers.

I learned to be a bar tender and it was a terrific experience. I met many big shots including Ray Hickcock who later founded the Young Presidents Organization. I worked several times at his family cottage at parties he gave. He even wrote a letter for me to the Cornell University Hotel Management School where I applied after two summers working in hotels. I thought that was a business I'd enjoy. However my grades weren't good enough to transfer and I couldn't afford Cornell anyway.

The kids I worked with were great fun and the parties practically every night at different places on the island were terrific for a party lover. I fell in love with a beautiful but goofy red headed Canadian who came to UNC to visit later that fall. We had a great time but her goofiness got old as she pushed to get married.

Tom Thomas and Erwin Potts were particularly good buddies that summer and we have stayed in touch over the years. I made contact with Erwin again when I saw his name on an annual report as chairman of McClatchy, one of the largest newspaper chains. He was very successful and we have visited and played golf on occasion. Tommy is retired and living in the Atlanta area. We had a reunion several years ago when Susie and I stayed with him and his wife, Bev.

Big Win Inn closed down after Labor Day each year. So for the two weeks before reporting back to UNC Tommy and I got a job at the Canadian National Exposition in Toronto. We stayed in the Phi Kappa Sigma house. I parked cars from 8:30 to noon then worked as a white-coated helper at Canada Packers food demonstration booth where I could eat well. I came home with $750 from tips and jobs in Canada—more money than I had ever had.

Much to my surprise on arriving back in Lincolnton I was met by Mom, Dad, and Jack and given a new Pontiac Catalina hardtop coupe, two-tone cream body and green top with leather seats—auto transmission and a hood ornament that was a small Indian (Pontiac) head that lit up red at night. (Mother called the car Rudolph, as in "the Red-Nosed Reindeer.") So I went back to UNC for my junior year with a neat new car. It cost $2,700, which was a whole lot then for my folks to pay. My dad never made more than $10,000 a year in his life.

The summer between my junior and senior year was taken up by six weeks of summer school. I had gotten a few D's and F's when I was very sick with mono and had to make up lost "quality points." An F was minus one point; D was zero points, C plus one point, B plus two and A plus three. Thanks to summer school and an extra effort senior year, I made enough A's and B's to graduate with a high C average in 1955. What a great time I had during my senior year! I was confident to the point of arrogance. I was popular, and I knew hundreds of students. I was a glad-handing sales type with a lot of street smarts from having lived a relatively unsheltered life.

My brother Jack was burning up law school. He was on the Law Review Board and was very popular too. He drove a new, white and green Roadmaster (4-holer) Buick Coupe, and wore great clothes from Milton's Clothing Cupboard Store. Milton Julian was a good friend of ours and we had both worked for him at different times. Jack also worked at the Buick dealership selling cars while he was in law school—we needed the money!

Jack and I graduated at the same time—he from law school and I from business school. I graduated with a bachelor of science in Industrial Relations, a degree in Labor/Management, which required fewer accounting and statistics courses, —courses in which I had done poorly when I was so sick. In addition, I'm sure I had attention deficit disorder before it became an excuse for not paying attention.

Throughout college, Jack had financial help from the GI bill and a working wife, so the monetary drain on our parents was lessened. I worked hard waiting tables in the frat house and selling clothes to generate my own spending money, but Mom and Dad were paying my tuition and room and board monthly. Their business was meager, and they looked forward to my financial independence.

After law school, Jack became extremely successful. He made a lot of money early. He lived in a fancy house with the best furniture and Lincoln automobiles. Over time he had a beach house, a lake house, a mountain house, a town house, boats, an airplane, and a large law firm. Unfortunately, he had trouble maintaining that high life. Eventually, he and his wife divorced, and his law partners left him. He regrouped to a small law firm for the rest of his life. There, he made much less than his style of living would suggest he had. He is deceased now. When I recall Jack I think of the times when he was an important mentor, giving me good advice about career choices. All in all he was a good big brother.

Jack had two very attractive children: his daughter Jacqueline was an outstanding student in college and became an MD. She lives in San Diego with her wonderful husband, Bob Wailes, also a doctor and good businessman. They have three lovely children and are very positive people. We stay in touch. They come to visit us from time to time. Jack's son Ron lives in North Carolina and is doing well.

BOB WAILES AND MY NIECE JACQUELYN HARRIS WAILES

8

Interview with Owens-Illinois

D uring my college days, Jack was always my adviser. When I told him I was thinking about going to law school, he said Mom and Dad couldn't afford more schooling costs. I didn't have the GI bill that he did, and my grades weren't great. He told me that taking a good corporate job could be just as rewarding as being a lawyer. "If you're good, you'll do well either place," he said.

During my last year of college I started making appointments with corporate recruiters who visited the campus. I had interviews with Colgate, Cargill, Owens-Illinois Glass Company, R. J. Reynolds, and several others.

Colgate was looking for people to work in their international Division, and I was very interested in that. I wanted to see the world. A popular song lyric back then was, "Far away places with strange sounding names / Far away over the sea . . . keep calling to me." (Those jukebox songs all seemed to have a personal message for me.) Colgate didn't want me. Cargill wanted me to consider working in a dog food plant of theirs. I thought that job didn't fit the image I had of myself as a sharp dresser with a sharp car—a sophisticated wannabe on the fringe of society. When I said I wasn't interested, my interviewer was upset. He thought UNC was not for Cargill. I don't know if they ever came back. I later learned how big and important Cargill was.

One afternoon, I was down in the basement bar of the Phi Kap house preparing for a party with a sorority when Wally O'Neal, Phi Kap president, asked me how my interviews were coming. I told him, and he said I should have signed up to talk with Owens-Illinois Glass Company. So I called up immediately, and there was an opening within an hour if I could make it to Carroll Hall, where the interview took place. I cleaned up, put on a serious suit, and went in with zero preparation about Owens-Illinois to meet with Ernie Marks from Toledo—a sparkling little man with a generous smile and manner that put me at ease as he explained what Owens-Illinois did. They were the biggest in glass bottles, glass building blocks, TV bulbs, pharmaceutical packaging, and scientific glassware for labs.

Having consumed and sold thousands of soft drinks in bottles at dad's gas station, I knew about duraglass (returnable) bottles and someone had said they were the "best." Ernie and I hit it off. While telling him about all my hustling at so many jobs growing up, he must have seen my drive and ambition. After explaining my poor sophomore grades as a combination of freshman and sophomoritis and mono, he said he thought I'd be a good prospect and that I'd be hearing from him. I did. He soon invited me to Toledo, Ohio for interviews.

The flight to Toledo was unforgettable. The thunder storms and lighting nearly blew us out of the sky before we landed at Willow Run, the old airport in Detroit. I flew with a frat pledge named David Smith from Adrian, Michigan. His parents picked us up at the airport and took me to the Commodore Perry Hotel in Toledo, where I stayed for two days of interviews.

Frankly, during the interviews, I didn't think my southern charm was working with a couple of key executives, and I was given a pretty short shrift by several of them who were too 'busy.' It looked as if I were going to strike out. Then I met Vice President of the Kimble Division Ben Dennis, as Ernie Marks and I were going to lunch on the elevators of the eleventh floor. Ben asked where I was from, and I told him North Carolina. He said he had been to Pinehurst golf course many times, and he asked if I had played there. I said I had with the UNC golf team (even though I wasn't really on the team and had only played with them at Pinehurst for fun). Wow! Ben brightened up and couldn't have been nicer when he thought I was a member of the golf team.

I got an offer to come to work for Owens-Illinois that afternoon as a salesman trainee at $325 a month—almost $4,000 a year. I didn't lie about the golf team. I just didn't make any effort to correct the great man's misinterpretation of my time with them. Golf has served me well! It wasn't until two or three years later, when he invited me to play Inverness with him and his son that I was forced to reveal the truth. By then, I was riding high as a promising employee for Kimble Glass Division of Owens-Illinois.

Tobacco companies were a large part of North Carolina's economy at that time. Textiles and furniture were also core businesses. My frat brother Joe Correll's father was one of the top personnel executives (now human resources) at R. J. Reynolds. Joe encouraged me to have an interview with his father and take an aptitude test. Since I was not an A student, I thought taking the test was just a losing drill. For some reason, I did very well on it. I got a call to come to Winston-Salem for an interview with—get this—Bowman Gray, chairman, and Francis Carter, president of R. J. Reynolds. I was too dumb to know that if I passed muster with these guys, I was a potential fast tracker with RJR.

Since I had a job with Owens-Illinois, I had more than my usual confidence and arrogance, and as this interview took place, I smoked. Everybody did in those days, if they were 'cool.' (I actually distributed sample Winston and Salem cigarettes for a year or more during college). So there he was, old Bowman Gray, sitting behind a 10-foot long desk—a little man who wheezed and coughed—and Francis Carter—a big, bald, bear of a man who deferred to Mr. Gray. There they sat interviewing me. Having been raised in a retail store selling tobacco of all types from cigarettes to snuff, I knew the routine of panel truck drivers setting up displays to promote brands, point of sale advertising, posters, and clocks. I knew the drivers, several of whom stayed at Ivy & Oaks, my family's 'motel,' I remember asking big league questions like "Mr. Gray, what do you do if cigarettes and tobacco in general go out of style?" I don't remember exactly what he said, but he didn't think that would happen. Even with my being a smart ass, I got an offer to come to work for RJR driving a panel truck and setting up displays for $250 per month. I told them I already had an offer for $325 from Owens-Illinois, and they said the cost of living up North made that even.

Once again, my ego and stupidity drove me—thank goodness! I would have died young if I had remained a smoker working for a tobacco company. Besides, I wanted to see more of the world—the United States, really—and didn't want to set up displays even for a short while. I wrote them a nice letter declining the offer.

Mr. Correll—Joe's father who had arranged the interview for me—nearly had a stroke at how dumb I was to turn down the offer. But I needed new boundaries, and North Carolina was pretty stagnant in those days. I took the Owens-Illinois offer and moved to Toledo, Ohio.

9

On the Corporate Ladder

I reported for work June 20, 1955, after a memorable beach party at Pauley's Island, South Carolina, with Dee Dee Davenport. Failing to receive a better offer from some NC blueblood, she asked me to come to her home and go to the party. Dee Dee hadn't gotten her MRS degree at Chapel Hill and was having a panic attack when she approached me in her cap and gown in the graduation line with the invitation. Let's just say that her parents were most pleasant as I spent one night in their Florence, South Carolina, home and attended the beach party. Most girls wanted to get married right after college—a ring with the degree—and it was ego-building for me (as if I needed it) to receive two letters from two other girls I had dated in college, asking me to come see them.

I drove to Toledo, Ohio, on June 19, 1955, and reported to a Mr. Walter Ardner, who gave me a small expense advance and pushed lots of paper at me to sign. It seemed like the rounds of visits to every division and department were endless. The head of each one tried to convince me that what he did was critical to Owens-Illinois' success. There was the Technical Center, Duraglas Center, Glass Container Division, and its many sales managers and assistants.

After a few weeks, I got my assignment to go to Vineland, New Jersey. This was Kimble's home plant where the glass tubing which was converted into vials, ampules, and containers for pills and injectable pharmaceuticals was produced. Glass tubing and rod had myriad applications, from thermometers to neon light tubes and glass rod towel bars. There was also a hand-blown operation that produced laboratory glassware in the same manner as was done hundreds of years ago. I went through every department, even the batch house, where a mixture of sand, soda, ash, and other ingredients was used to make glass of various types. There are many types of glass (like Pyrex) that have different chemical compatibilities resulting in resistance to chemicals and heat. Myriad colors and strength are possible.

Pharmaceutical glass is Type I, a borosilicate glass that does not leach mineral materials like regular lime glass. I was really fascinated with the processes and technology as I stood around the 2,500 degree heat of glass furnaces and fabricating machines. I was in Vineland for two and a half months, got along well with the factory people and received good reports regarding my sales ability. One day while there, several of the hot shot New York branch office salesmen came to Vineland. I was introduced to Fred Elder, a fast-talking, charming salesman who had made a mark as a World War II pilot. He became my 'big brother' when I was assigned to the New York branch office. He would later work for me at AIM Packaging.

As the training program progressed, I was called back to Toledo in the fall of 1955 for more instruction at headquarters. South Jersey had been fun with its beaches, golf courses, and down-to-earth people. In Toledo, I joined a group of student trainees consisting of George Grosshans of Dartmouth, Warren Yetter, a Toledoan from Harvard Business School, Bob Latta of Missoula, Montana and the University of Montana, and two others.

One thing I found as I started with Owens-Illinois: I could golf better than most of the salesmen. Many of them were returning from military duty and were, like me, fighting their way up the economic ladder. In that environment, I was regarded as an outstanding golfer, which I was not, but I was very pleased to be considered so.

10

Susie

After a few days of training at HQ in Toledo, I asked Warren Yetter if he knew any girls we could date. He set up a Saturday night dinner for six of us at the Old Plantation Inn in Maumee with his wife-to-be, Susan Dudley, George and Phyllis Grosshans, and a blind date for me—Susie Draper. Susie's parents had just moved into a beautiful home on the Maumee River, so I was pretty impressed with their assets when I picked up Miss Draper for dinner. She was quiet and reserved as we broke the ice discussing where we were from, what college we had attended, and career plans.

We met the others at the restaurant. Susie was cool, poised, and very attractive. They were all Ivy League types. Harvard, Dartmouth, Vassar, and Radcliff were their common grounds for Eastern private schools. Grand plans for success seemed guaranteed by all these smart and attractive people. I quickly tried to join the conversation by telling about my one trip to New York City and what a great time I had at the University of North Carolina, drawling in my molasses southern talk. The page turned quickly as they all discussed their trips to Europe and all that they had seen and done there.

I watched quietly as everyone else enjoyed the evening. However, when I took Susie home and was saying goodnight at the door, the handshake was as sensuous as a handshake could be.

After a few days, I called Susie to see if she would like to go to a movie and have dinner. I didn't know anyone else, and she was very attractive. After dinner and a movie she seemed more interested in me, but nothing clicked—a little kiss goodnight, and I thought, "This ain't going to work!"

Then, in desperation a week later, I called her again, and she asked if I would like to go with her to the Ohio State/University of Michigan football game in Ann Arbor the next Saturday. Her sister, Donna, and husband-to-be, Peter Burr, were in school there. Well, that was an easy answer: Oh, yeah! It was a great Saturday in Big Ten country and we had fun. We drank a few and then I drove home to Maumee/Toledo with my arm around her. We parked behind the barn and were doing some serious kissing when her father, wielding a flashlight, broke things up, asking if everything was all right.

Things got pretty steady, and we started talking about a long-term relationship after Thanksgiving and Christmas parties in Toledo, Perrysburg, and Maumee. I met many of her friends and passed the 'sniff test,' at least marginally. Her parents were less than impressed with ol' south mouth, but they were always very nice to me.

11

Romance Blooms

S o there I was, in love but nearly broke. I borrowed cash from the Owens-Illinois credit union to fly home to North Carolina for Christmas. Brother Jack was doing well in a law practice with Mr. Robert Collier, his son, Bob, and four or five others in Statesville, North Carolina. My mom and dad were having tough economic times and were watching every cent—never complaining, either. I asked my brother how you know when love is the real thing. Jack said, "When you just want to be with someone doing anything, or nothing." That fit the situation. I believed Susie felt the same about me.

After Christmas and New Year's Eve, 1956, we were wondering how things could work out. She was a Vassar liberal arts major in Russian, and I was a salesman-to-be. All of a sudden—Bam! I got the choice assignment to report to the New York City branch office on the 48th floor of the Chrysler Building, working for Mr. Ed Bowes. That was the branch where Fred Elder, Lou Ross, Erv Norton, Dan Glesser, and John McGuire were the best and brightest salesmen of the Kimble Division. I even got a raise of $50 per month. Little did I know I would have needed $150 more to break even in NYC.

I shared an apartment with Jim Irwin, a glass-container salesman. We had twin beds in a two-room apartment in Tudor City, which was on 1st Avenue across from the United Nations and within walking distance of the Chrysler Building. The learning curve was straight up while I applied my training and made some sales.

I traveled mostly with Fred Elder, whom I watched with awe as he said the right things on the job, with wit and also concern that the customer was happy. I eventually got my own list of accounts to call on- all 200 to 300 of them. Few of them were active customers. Most were 'cats and dogs' with no worthwhile business and bad credit. Many were immigrants who barely spoke English. They thought I certainly didn't speak English either with my southern drawl. Glass towel bars were my biggest dollar items, sold through retail chain stores (which are all now long gone). Calling on them was a cram session in two-year-old magazines in the waiting room for one to two hours. Then some surly SOB gave me five or 10 minutes to talk about towel bars. One minute was more than enough. All they wanted to know was the price.

I learned the subway system from Grand Central to all over Manhattan and to Brooklyn, Queens, the Bronx, and part of New Jersey. It's said that a good New Yorker never has to go out into the rain.

I wrote reports on so many dead accounts that I felt like a business undertaker. I did dig up a good customer in Forest Hills, Queens, called Speedry Products owned by Dr. Schindel. He invented the first felt tip magic marker in a small two-ounce glass vial for pills but it was very expensive. I sold him a private bottle mold for $2,500 and saved him $10,000 the first year. Then, it boomed to a big account. I got a raise to $500 per month after pleading poverty to Ben Dennis and Ken Hewitt—Toledo bosses who came to NYC mostly to drink and party, as far as I could tell. My biggest deal back then was trying to convince General Foods in White Plains that they should package Maxwell House Coffee in a Type One glass carafe that could be used as a decanter for hot coffee. Type One glass is like Pyrex (a Corning brand). However, one order for this would have sold out the entire Chicago Heights plant of Kimble, the only bottle plant we had making Type One for pharmaceutical serum bottles (small ones at high prices). So we had to pass on the coffee container, but it got top management attention in Toledo. Boy, was I digging to make a mark as NYC expenses kept me really hungry!

While scratching to get into the so-called big leagues of selling in NYC I stayed in touch with my love, Susie, except when she went with her parents to the Caribbean for two or three weeks. On her return, she decided to come to New York City to look for a job, hoping to use her Russian language major from Vassar. She was good and vetted for security, but she wasn't good enough for the UN. (She had planned to go to Washington, D.C., but changed that to be with me, as our love bloomed.) She moved in with some classmates from Vassar who rented an apartment on 9th Street in Greenwich Village between 5th and 6th Avenues. It was Judy, Carol, Tandy, and one more. She got the cot in the living room, behind a screen—very un-private!

Her job hunting was not going well and I was afraid she was going to go elsewhere, when a classmate friend from UNC, Bob Hoffman, turned up at a party. He worked in personnel at McGraw-Hill Publishing and set up an interview for her. She got hired in the Textbook Sales Division working in the old Green Building on West 42nd Street.

So there we were, seeing as much as we could of each other in Manhattan, standing up at Broadway shows, riding the Staten Island Ferry, walking in Central Park, going to movies, doing lots of hugging and kissing as our love deepened. Then, in the spring of 1956, she came down with mono, the same kissing disease I had in college, and was very sick with a high fever. Her parents came to New York from Toledo and unceremoniously took her home to get well.

12

Marriage

We had talked about getting married, and Susie persuaded her parents that I was the guy. So around May of 1956, she got their consent and things moved fast. We went to Lincolnton, North Carolina, to meet my folks that spring. In June Mom and Dad flew to Toledo to meet the Drapers. I arrived from New York City. As my parents were getting to know the Drapers I took Susie into another room, presented her with the engagement ring which I had borrowed money to buy. I "officially" asked her to marry me and she said "Yes!" She was thrilled and so was I. The Drapers gave a lovely party inviting many of their friends to celebrate the occasion.

My wedding to Virginia Welles Draper was set for September 29, 1956, in Maumee, Ohio. (My wife's nickname, Susie, was given to her by the family maid, Mamie Gray. When she was born, they couldn't figure out what to name her because she was supposed to have been William, her father's first name. So the maid started calling her "little Susie" which stuck and remained even after she was named Virginia.)

My wedding was a big deal for my family and me as we descended on Toledo—Mom with a very bad back problem, Dad with his southern accent so thick everyone thought his name was "Hass" instead of "Harris," Aunt Virginia in her finest clothes, and brother Jack suave and cool as he charmed everyone with his smooth talk.

We had parties and luncheons, presents, and toasts every noon and

OUR WEDDING PICTURE, SEPTEMBER 29, 1956

night. Susie's father, William C. Draper, was a very handsome, distinguished man of high rank in the Toledo Trust Company bank. The Drapers knew everyone worth knowing in Toledo, and many of them were there at our beautiful ceremony at St. Paul's Episcopal Church and at the reception in perfect weather, in a lovely tent at their home on the river. What an event, worthy of many more words to describe how beautiful, but of great relief for me to get off the stage because I was a nervous wreck.

The wedding trip honeymoon was to have been a stay in the Pocono Mountains on our way back to New York City to report for work in a few days. But Mr. Draper had set up reservations at the Otsego Club in Gaylord, Michigan, so that's where we went after the first night at the Dearborn Inn in Dearborn, Michigan. We were so tired and so in love, a sleeping bag would have been just fine. We arrived at Otsego Lodge, 200 miles north, and settled into the bridal suite, canopied bed and all, at a cottage for about three or four days. Love was grand, and the weather was beautiful with fall leaf colors at their peak. We drove to Leland to see her family cottage and ate at little restaurants here and there. I nearly panicked when I read on the back of the cottage room door that the rate was $70 per day. I was in debt for the ring and other costs and hoped my money would hold out until we got back to New York. However, upon checkout, I learned the Drapers had paid for the cottage as a wedding present, among others. What a relief, and how thoughtful and nice of them!

After our honeymoon, Susie and I went back to Maumee. We packed up most of our wedding presents for storage and took some with us back to New York. Before we left, I'll never forget Mr. Draper, whose nickname was Biggie, saying to me, "Think big, Frank, think big." That was certainly a bit of advice that would come in handy and serve me well later, as I put it into practice.

We lived in Tudor City in the apartment I had shared with Jim Irvin who had served as a groomsman in our wedding. Owens-Illinois had transferred him to a different location for a while. After a few months there, we moved to Mount Vernon in West Chester County into a cheaper Wildwood Gardens apartment, where there was a place to park the car.

OUR WEDDING
INVITATION

Mr. and Mrs. William Corlett Draper

request the pleasure of your company

at the wedding reception of their daughter

Virginia Welles
and
Mr. Francis Meetze Harris

on Saturday, the twenty-ninth of September

at four o'clock

1714 River Road

Maumee, Ohio

The favour of a reply is requested

NEWLY MARRIED

SUSIE AND
HER FATHER,
"BIGGIE" DRAPER

FRONT, L-R JIM IRWIN, BROTHER JACK, MY BEST MAN,
FRANK HARRIS, DAD (WALTER); BACK, L-R GEORGE
GROSSHANS, DAVE MCCLEAN, BILL LATHROP

BRIDE'S MAIDS, L-R DONNA DRAPER BURR, MAID OF
HONOR, DELIA WALBRIDGE, SUSIE THOMAS GUINEVERE,
JUDY GREGORY BOWES, SUE DORNBLAZER

VIEW FROM RIVER-FRONT YARD OF HOME WHICH
WAS WELLES, THEN DRAPER AND THEN HARRIS

THE BIG WEDDING RECEPTION TENT WITH VIEWS OF THE RIVER

"LET THEM EAT CAKE"

WITH BROTHER JACK AND MALCOLM WARD, THE EPISCOPAL PRIEST

L-R MAE WELLES, SUSIE'S GRANDMOTHER, PINKIE HARRIS,
FRANK'S MOTHER, AND VIRGINIA DOGAN, FRANK'S AUNT

SUSIE AND GRANDMOTHER WELLES

SUSIE WITH
SISTER DONNA

SUSIE WITH
HER MOTHER,
"TOOKIE"

SETTING UP THE RECEPTION UNDER THE BIG TENT

13

On Up the Ladder

The office was moved from the Chrysler Building to Montclair, New Jersey, and I got reassigned to the Chicago, Illinois office to "take on more responsible accounts" in May of 1957. Susie and I found a place to live in Winnetka, Illinois at Long Meadow Farm on the corner of Hibbard and Illinois Roads. Two neighboring couples, Tom and Peg Waldridge and Don and B. L. Moyle, have remained friends over the years. I reported to Bruce Puffer, branch manager in the Civic Opera Building to get my review of Chicago and my account assignments. The accounts were hundreds of cats and dogs—not bigger accounts, as I expected—that bought very little, if ever, and were scattered from Milwaukee to St. Louis. I was upset, but away I went, trying to find that pony in the pile of manure, while wearing out the Pontiac driving through Chicago traffic and endless cornfields to Springfield, Kankakee, and Rockford. There were no company cars then. You used your own and got 10 cents per mile. I made some small successes but learned to hate Bruce Puffer, who knew everything about everything and sat in his office with the door closed, doing what, none of us knew.

After nine months of frustration, I called Ernie Marks, who had recruited me. When I said I was going to quit, he said, "Wait. Let me try something else." After meeting with Henry Rudy in Corporate Marketing, I got offered a job in Merchandising back in the Toledo

Duraglass Center, trying to help glass container salesmen do better selling closures and plastic fitments for bottles. Closure & Plastics was a
small division under $50 million, but I was there in HQ meeting the big
shots, as I learned how to write presentations and even speeches for the
VPs. There was a bunch of us doing this for various sections of Owens-
Illinois—glass, paper, and prescription packages. John Clement, Sam
Downs, Jack Schaffer, and several others were sharp big picture think-
ers who taught me the role of marketing, from manufacturing and con-
sumption to disposal of the package (now recycling).

After Susie and I came back from the Chicago area, we lived on
Inwood Place in Maumee, Ohio, only a mile or so from where her par-
ents lived. Susie was pregnant with our first child, Virginia Draper
Harris, who was born September 6, 1958, at Flower Hospital in
Toledo.

All of us from each division were pulled in to help promote glass
bottles for soft drinks and beer nationwide. Cans were taking most of
the market away from the traditional returnable glass bottles and the
non-refundable bottles. I came up with the idea to make a short, fat,
light-weight glass container that I called "The Glass Can." Old management struggled to accept the fact that the metal can was preferred
for many reasons including space savings throughout the distribution
channels from boxes, trucks, and shelves, to coolers. We, as a company and as an industry, embarked on a multi-million dollar promotion
of the Glass Can, which, we claimed, protected the flavor better, and
filled almost as fast as metal cans. What a crock of hope and waste of
time and money! Cans continued to take 80 percent of the market. But
I learned an important lesson: don't bet on losers, when the evidence
is against you. If the competition's product is better, less costly, more
consumer friendly and available, don't start a losing war.

14

Plastic Bottles at Owens-Illinois

Owens-Illinois had been one of the first producers of plastic bottles back in the late 1940s and '50s. The company developed a joint venture with Monsanto (Plax), one of the suppliers of plastic closure liners for glass bottles and other materials, to produce low density poly-bottles that found a market for nasal sprays, underarm deodorants, and other small volume special applications where the 'squeeze' function was important. The business was small in dollar value.

Then in the late '50s, high density polyethylene (HDPE) was developed by several chemical companies: Phillips Petroleum, W. R. Grace, Union Carbide, and some overseas companies. This material was much more rigid and stiff and had much better barrier properties to contain the products adequately.

Around 1956 or '57, Owens-Illinois sold its 50 percent interest in Plax to Monsanto and proceeded to develop and refine the BC-3 machines to produce a wide range of bottle sizes and shapes. The Plastic Bottle Division was formed under George Babcock, and in 1959 I got invited to be its first salesman, assigned to New York City: back to the Chrysler Building, 47th floor this time, again reporting to Jim Bargman. He had been a glass salesman who was appointed as one of four or five new plastic products district managers around the

United States for this new division. Jim was a nice guy but, needless to say, the Glass Division didn't give up its best people to staff these jobs, and the learning curve for all of us was vertical as new materials and new machines to produce bottles and decorate them with labels were developed at warp speed. The world of packaging was in revolution! Glass and metal containers were under siege from plastic and still are as this is written 50 years later. Eventually, I predict that glass containers will all be replaced by plastic because of the economics, convenience, safety, light weight, and ease of dispensing. Look at ketchup bottles. Old materials die hard, and it took a generation to learn that plastics are good, not evil, as they were portrayed by ignorant and aggressive environmentalists.

In 1959 Susie and I were back in New York. We found a house for around $27,000 in Riverside, Connecticut, with air-conditioning, which was a rare commodity in those days in private homes. It required an enormous amount of remodeling and redecorating in order to make it livable. We settled into the remodeling mode in my spare time, and with a very small child, we stayed home a lot.

I began to work the territory with Jim Bargman and proceeded with the effort to develop some sales for plastic bottles. Jim handled most of the big accounts like Colgate, Lever Brothers, American Home Products, and Johnson & Johnson, where he was able to develop the first plastic baby powder container. Once again, I handled the development accounts, but plenty of them were large enough to make everything very worthwhile.

It was about this time that I had the opportunity to go on my first duck hunt on Long Island Sound, not too far from our home in Connecticut. I went out to one of the islands on the sound with Bill Arata, who was married to Susie Thomas, my wife's best friend. I had not killed one duck when the game warden came by and discovered I didn't have a hunting license.

Bill said to the game warden, "This is a real rookie. He didn't know enough to get a license, and I loaned him the gun."

The game warden said, "Well, Mr. Harris, why don't you just go find that license that you forgot to bring with you. Meet me at Saugatuck at the end of the day, and we'll see if we can avoid paying the charge ($75) for not having a license."

So I ran over the whole area around Greenwich, Connecticut, and finally found a license and a duck stamp, which cost about $20. That was a lot of money for me in those days. I raced up to Saugatuck at dark and showed it to the warden. He said, "All right, Mr. Harris, I'll tear this ticket up." That was a great lesson. I was never without the proper credentials for shooting again.

As it turned out, my sales efforts in New York, New Jersey, and Long Island didn't last very long because I was promoted nine months later to be the district manager in Baltimore, Maryland, for the Plastic Products Division. We moved to Baltimore in the spring of 1960. At this point I had moved six times counting the first assignment to NYC—then five more times with Susie in five years. I spent the next five years in Baltimore as district manager. That title really meant that I was a salesman with a secretary, an administrative assistant, and later on another salesman to help me. It was my first management job. It was

OUR HOUSE ON SUMMER HILL DR., PHOENIX MARYLAND, IN
1960 WHEN I BECAME DISTRICT MANAGER IN BALTIMORE

a small one, but I was excited. We sold our home in Connecticut for a profit of $3,000 or so and bought a house in Summer Hill Developments, a lovely area of Maryland, overlooking the Loch Raven Reservoir. It was a back-to-front split level house in Williamsburg colors and design—only fair construction, but charming architectural features. I loved that area, especially Chesapeake Bay for hunting reasons.

On December 2, 1960, our son, Walter Corlett Harris, was born in Woman's Hospital in Baltimore. We were delighted to have a son. Walter was my father's name and Corlett was Susie's father's middle name. Both Susie's parents and mine came to see the new addition to the family.

After buying our home in Phoenix, which is north of Baltimore, I found that I had to commute most of the time to Philadelphia. That's where I should have been assigned in the first place. The only business that we had in Baltimore was McCormick Tea & Spice, which had already been established before I got there. I developed Mangles Herold, another good-sized account, and a couple of other bleach bottle accounts. We had a plastic bottle plant that was put into service primarily for Proctor and Gamble, which was handled out of our Cincinnati office.

The weekly trip back and forth to Philadelphia was through very pretty, historic country. The pharmaceutical companies of Merck Sharp & Dome, SmithKline & French, Wyeth Laboratories, Sterling Drug, and others were located in the Philadelphia area. I had a great deal of success in the conversion of pill and capsule containers—which are called dry pharmaceuticals—into polyethylene bottles from the amber, green, or clear glass bottles used in the past. It was really a pretty easy process to convert them. The biggest problem was with the filling lines and labeling operations. Plastic bottles provided great savings in weight and space, and, of course, there's the breakage issue with glass. I sold the advantages of plastic successfully. It really set me apart as a specialist in pharmaceutical containers.

Susie and I found the Baltimore area wonderful. It was far enough south that I could feel very comfortable with the people there, as opposed to the New York City drill. I worked with glass container

Branch Manager Ned Morse, who, along with his wife, Eleanor, became good friends. Ned was very helpful to me. He had a group of about five salesmen reporting to him for handling the glass beverage bottles and every other kind of glass bottles for food, beer, and liquor. He invited me to play golf at various Maryland clubs and introduced me to important people.

I was being terribly underpaid, making somewhere under $12,000 a year. But I had a company car, and Susie had the turquoise and white 1957 Chevrolet station wagon that we bought in Chicago. That turned out to be one of the great classic cars of all time. We used it extensively.

Also, while in the Baltimore area, we had the opportunity to do enjoyable things with my friend, Fred Elder, who at that time was the plant manager of the Vineland, New Jersey plant only a couple of hours away. He had a sailboat on Chesapeake Bay where we spent weekends with him and his wife, Phyllis, from time to time.

I got seriously interested in goose hunting and duck hunting on the eastern shores of Maryland around Graysonville, which is just across the bay bridge. I hunted with an old curmudgeon of a guide named

DUCK HUNTING, CIRCA 1966. TO MY LEFT ARE
TOM SWIGART AND JACK HARRIS.

GOOSE HUNT CIRCA 1963, EASTERN SHORE, MARYLAND. L-R,
BROTHER JACK, FRANK HARRIS, GEORGE URSCHEL, BOB EBERT,
TOM SWIGART, SKIP GIFFORD AND CHARLES MCKELVY

Pete Beecher and his two sons. We entertained many customers in
those days with hunting and fishing and I eventually leased a farm on
Kent Island for my friends and family. We had lots of fun working to
fix up the blinds. Hunting was a hot button for both the general manager of the Plastics Products Division, George Babcock, and the general sales manager, Jim Rudy, who would come down to Maryland to
be entertained along with our customers at hunting as well as eating
the good eastern shore fish and crabs.

As a strange aside, my boss at Owens-Illinois, Dan McIver, and I
were on Chesapeake Bay shooting ducks the day that John Kennedy
was killed in Dallas. Dan was going to go to fly back to Toledo out of
the Washington Baltimore airport, but he had his gun with him. I said
"Maybe you better leave this gun down here in Maryland with me until
things settle down." Curiously enough, five years later I was sitting in
a restaurant in Cincinnati, Ohio, with Dan again, when the word came
that Martin Luther King had been killed. Dan turned to me and said,

"We've got to stop meeting. They are killing off too many important people when we are together."

In the late spring of 1965 I had been district manager in Baltimore for five years. At a division meeting at the Ponte Vedra Club in Florida, I was taken aside by Jim Rudy and George Babcock for a private conversation. They said there was a reorganization taking place and that they would like me to come back to Toledo and be a product group manager for the pharmaceutical, toiletry, and cosmetic industries. I would be reporting to Jim Rudy.

I had previously said to them, if they were going to do anything different with me, do it pretty soon because I was getting my roots down in Baltimore and had some other job opportunities there. I hoped that they would get on with promotions if that was going to happen. So it did happen, and I was very excited about going back to Toledo with a title that at least sounded important enough to assuage my ego, which was not shrinking.

15

Back to Toledo

Susie and I bought a gorgeous Victorian house in a great location in Perrysburg, Ohio. It was over 100 years old, with 12-foot ceilings, four bedrooms, and a fantastic living room big enough to hold a square dance. It had been remodeled and redecorated by several other executives of Owens Corning before us. It was next to one of the top people at Owens-Illinois and there were other major executives of Owens Corning and Owens-Illinois in the neighborhood.

While we enjoyed our lovely home and being back in the Toledo area, it was not financially rewarding at first. I had to give up my company car in exchange for a $75 a month raise. But then I had to buy another car to commute to work. I found a five-year-old Volkswagen convertible that was cheap and fun.

When we arrived in Toledo in 1965 from Maryland, Susie's mother had been seriously ill with throat cancer. She died in 1966. We sadly watched her terrible downward spiral, her suffering with cancer, the radiation treatments, and all that she went through. She was a lovely person who lost her battles with cancer.

Jim Rudy, my boss, was a fun, eccentric Yale graduate from Paducah, Kentucky. He loved to hunt and fish, and he was superb at it. He was one of the best shooters I've ever seen. He was a somewhat phlegmatic guy who spoke in absolutes most of the time, never in doubt about anything, generally a very pleasant guy to be with. He was deferential to

F. R. MILLER HOUSE AT 241 EAST FRONT (BUILT C. 1872). A classic Italianate structure built by a German-born merchant who came here in 1850, this home has the typical roof cresting and incised stone lintels over tall, narrow windows. Single brackets are beneath the wide roof overhang that is decorated with dentils. The double front door has arched panes with a floral etched transom. The original carriage house in the rear has matching patterns. Miller was a lieutenant colonel and commandant of Fort McHenry in Baltimore during the Civil War. He was also a mayor of Perrysburg.

ELABORATE FRONT PORTICO. The unique feature of this home is the elaborate front portico—all covered in stamped tin. The ornamental columns have thick composite capitals, topped by a balustrade.

OUR PERRYSBURG HOUSE WHICH WE BOUGHT IN 1965 FOR $40,000. IT WAS A FIXER UPPER, MOST OF WHICH I DID.

PADDLE TENNIS AT THE TOLEDO COUNTRY CLUB

George Babcock, the corporate vice president of the division. George was a Princeton graduate, a good dresser and an articulate guy. I spent a lot of my time talking with Babcock, as opposed to Rudy, who was very unclear about what kind of direction he wanted to give me. I remember asking Rudy after I reported to him, "Well, boss, what do you have in mind for me to do as product group manager for these pharmaceutical and toiletry and cosmetics industries?"

His answer was, "I think you ought to plan to travel out of the Detroit Airport because the connections are an awful lot better than they are out of the Toledo airport."

That was about the extent of my directions as we embarked on a program to develop machines that were more competent to produce small drug bottles and bottles for toiletries and cosmetics, my new domain. We had a big development center with scores of people and a great big budget to develop new machines that were supposed to compete with those on the market and produced by others. I had a lot to do with engineering and material testing because plastics have such flexible applications. They have different properties, different appearances, and different characteristics from the standpoint of the ability to contain and protect products. We had to allow for the breakage resistance differing in all temperatures, and how to package products so that they weren't squashed from the weight of stacks in warehouses.

Owens-Illinois had become enormously successful, primarily in the glass bottle business where it had around 50% of the national market. The first automatic glass bottle blowing machine was developed by Mike Owens in the 1920s. With that, Owens Bottle Machine Company and the Illinois Glass Company merged and then took over many smaller companies to create the biggest glass packaging company in the world at that time. They had visions of doing the same thing with plastic bottles, with machines that would make them better and faster, as had been their experience in glass. Owens-Illinois tried to get patents on everything so that they could preclude the usual competition. Unfortunately it didn't work for plastic bottles.

Owens-Illinois and Owens Corning each had private fishing and hunting clubs for entertaining customers. Millsite Farms was owned by Preston Levis, president at Owens-Illinois, and Sunny Brook, Owens Corning's. Castalia Farms was different from the Castalia Fishing Club, originally owned by the first chairman of the board of Owens-Illinois, the founder, William Levis. Fishing in those areas was so very different from when I learned to fish in a poor little branch down in North Carolina. This was the big leagues with big league fishermen. They discussed fishing all over the country and the world: the Rocky Mountains, the Eastern streams of the Catskills and other parts of New England, New Zealand, and South America. Of course that whet my appetite to do it too.

The travel was extensive. I had wanted to the see the U.S. and boy, I sure did! Entertaining customers and associates was done in style as I was on an expense account. I was in New York at least once a month and in every other part of the United States, every place there was business to be developed. I traveled all the time, primarily with the district managers, all of whom I had known when I was one of them as it was a pretty small division. We were not very successful in making very much money and although we tried repeatedly to develop the machinery and utilize the capacity of the 10 or 12 plants that had been built over the previous six or seven years, we were still doing only $50 million to $60 million a year. We also had a lot of people who didn't really know what they were doing as managers. We had huge quality and service problems. We were slow on engineering. It took forever to get a set of production molds built. Sometimes, it could take a month to even get a price quote. Then there were the quality problems once the mold was built to get the bottle at the right dimensions and the right strength without revision after revision.

We were having problems with bottle-making machines other than the first machines that we developed, called the BC-3, and those had many limitations. All the new machines, the BC-5s, the BC-6s, the BC-7s on which we spent upwards of $10 million, failed. None of them was competent to produce good quality bottles at acceptable costs and speeds. We thought we had what we needed: a lot of supernumeraries in the division, everybody had a secretary, everybody had assistants, we were traveling, we were entertaining, and we were hoping that we could 'buy the business,' as we had in the past, with our personalities. But that didn't work very well any more because the competition was getting tougher and tougher.

Shortly after moving back to the Toledo area, my father-in-law invited me to go to Norway to fish for salmon at the very famous Mallingfoss Pool. It was a wonderful experience. Biggie, as my father-in-law was called, was also president of the Toledo Country Club. Up until then I had only played customer golf at public places or with friends who belonged to country clubs (to which I aspired). Now I was able to join the Toledo Country Club. Belonging to a country club was not only a great sport experience, but it also enabled my getting to know the people I wanted to know socially: the top management of Owens-Illinois. When I finally got into the economic echelon where it was possible to play, I played a lot.

We tried all the usual entertainment tactics, but this time whether we were entertaining them with trout fishing at Millsite and Castalia Farms or at shooting preserves, or going salmon fishing in Iceland, nothing seemed to work. All the fishing and hunting, the golf trips, dinners, and theatre were all overdone to try to sell our product, because our quality problems negated any of the things we did.

16

Losing Dad and Mom

Using a riding mower turned out to be one of my father's greatest joys in his later years, as he mowed the four acres of lawn at their home. But Dad had a horrible accident after he retired.

Foolishly, he filled the lawn mower using a glass gallon jug of gasoline. One day, he dropped it down the outside basement stairwell, and it shattered and threw gas everywhere. When he went down the stairs and opened the basement door to get a broom to sweep up the mess, a gas hot water heater's pilot light ignited the fumes and trapped him in the stairwell, where he could have burned to death. Mother saved him. He was terribly burned over 80 percent of his body. It's amazing he survived after all the plastic surgery and skin grafts. He was awfully crippled after that. Mother took care of him for another eight to 10 years before he passed away in June 1971 at 75 of lung cancer. He was a heavy smoker most of his life.

A year or two later, mother sold our home in Lincolnton. Taking her little poodle, she moved to Charlotte, two doors away from my Aunt Sarah. Her little house in Charlotte had a nice garden, and with her talents and charm she was very popular in the neighborhood. Mother was able to get along well with stipends that my brother and I sent, complementing her social security and meager savings. She lived there for about five years, and then my brother suggested she move to Statesville, where he was living with his new wife, Paulette. My mother moved into a small house there and it was a joy to see her having a happy existence in the same town as my brother and his children. She was a very attractive woman who dressed beautifully. She was actually a model at some of the stores and country club events as she had a beautiful figure well into her later years.

She passed away on December 11, 1988, two days before her 85th birthday. She was undergoing bypass surgery after having had some mild heart attacks. She was a very happy person to be around and we all miss her.

MY MOM AT THE WALDORF ASTORIA ON HER TRIP TO NEW YORK CITY

MY DAD AND MOM WITH WALTER AND GINGI WHEN THEY CAME TO SEE US IN OHIO, CIRCA 1969. WE TOOK THEM BACK TO THEIR OLD DETROIT NEIGHBORHOOD.

17

Trouble Brewing and a Way Out

The plastic products division was not making enough money to satisfy top management. The efforts to continue using machines and technology developed only by Owens-Illinois was a great inhibitor of our progress as other companies decided to get into the plastic bottle business. Many of those were the chemical companies that made the raw materials and the oil companies that made the feed stock for the chemical companies. They looked at the billions upon billions of bottles that were used, and they thought it would be a good opportunity to 'down stream' integrate and make more money than by just supplying raw materials.

Numerous companies started making plastic bottles. Among them were Phillips Petroleum, Monsanto, Ethyl's Imco Division, Shell Oil, Standard Oil, Union Carbide, Tenneco, and Celanese. It seemed as if everyone wanted to get in on the act. We were competing with larger companies with more knowledge about plastic materials, using machines, some that were far better than ours, that were produced by someone else—not in-house like Owens-Illinois. Some of them were also total flops. Tenneco spent tens of millions of dollars trying to develop a machine that never worked very well. But there were European machinery companies who moved quicker than we did in our own country to develop plastic bottle machines, specifically, the Bekum Company of West Germany. The Fischer Company made excellent machines, and they were being used by some of our competitors, particularly in the industries for which I was responsible.

In desperation, I investigated these machines on behalf of Owens-Illinois. I then put us in the queue to buy four Bekum machines and I actually had them sold out, based on their projected capacity. Four of them would cost $1 million for the basic machines, and would require about another million dollars for support equipment such as grinders, blenders, and conveyers to handle the capacity. I ordered it all without the authority from top management of the corporation but with knowledge of management in the division who agreed, as long as we could cancel the order. These machines were in great demand and since they required six to nine months to build, if we didn't take them, somebody else would. We then had to develop the presentation to top management to get the necessary $2 million. I already had enough bottle orders for clear polyvinylchloride (PVC), a fairly new plastic bottle material to fill the machines' productive capacity. PVC made it possible to package all the colors and contain the fragrance of toiletries and cosmetics, particularly shampoos

As it happened, a new boss, Mal Cooper, had come into the division. Jim Rudy was sidelined. I should have got Rudy's job because I knew more about plastic bottles, machinery, applications, and customers than anybody else—certainly in the company, if not in the world. Mal Cooper was a good-looking political type who had come from the international division and knew little about plastics. When he went to make the presentation to top management, he was given a very hard time about not making enough money with the machines we had. They asked him, "Why should Owens-Illinois invest in more new machinery that they don't know anything about?" He did such a lousy job of presenting it that he came back from the meeting and said, "They turned me down." We didn't get the capital to do it.

To say the least, I was absolutely flabbergasted that this occurred, after having worked my tail off with many customers, including Helene Curtis, Proctor & Gamble, Colgate, and many others to get the orders and buy the machines. I had to go and explain to customers that we had declined to buy these machines and give them their money back for the molds that we had been in the process of building. The mold money was not a huge amount, but the disappointment of not being able to receive bottles when they needed them for their marketing plans infuriated them. I did this as well as it could be done, trying to save my personal reputation in an industry where I was well-liked and knew just about everybody worth knowing.

Having done all this selling for so many years, it made me sick to disappoint customers. I gave this situation a great deal of thought, and, when I came back from my travels, I picked up the phone and called Bob Drury, who was running the Bekum Machine Company of Germany. I said, "Hold on. We got turned down, but I've got another idea, and I'm sure we can come up with a way to take delivery of those machines within the next three to four months. Besides that, you're not going to be deprived if we don't take them now because I know you've got other customers who will take them off your hands instantly." We had gotten to be pretty good friends, so he held the machines for me.

I decided that since they brought Mal Cooper in to be the general sales manager and I had lost that opportunity, it was time to move on. Mal had begun bringing in people from the International Division. They were all very attractive, politically astute people, most of whom didn't know squat about plastics and were more impressed with how they all dressed and talked than they were about having knowledge of the industry. They brought with them the old Owens-Illinois philosophy of "Well, let's just sell our charm and our bigness."

I was not a political ass-kisser, and I had not been given what I thought were adequate wages. So, what do you do next?

I flew down to North Carolina to talk with Mr. Bob Ebert, the son of the founder of Rubbermaid who had retired to be an investor. I met him through my brother, who was his next door neighbor in Statesville. A few years before when I was trying to figure out what to do with my life, Bob and I had looked at businesses, exploring the possibility of going into business together. We got along very well. We had tried to buy some injection molding businesses, vacuum forming businesses, and small plants around the North. I wanted to stay in Toledo if I could; we had a home there and lots of friends that we enjoyed.

I made a presentation to Ebert on a yellow legal pad about what these machines cost, what I could sell the product for, and what margins I believed we could make. He was very interested. I brought him a bunch of container samples representing the markets that we could satisfy. He was interested in going into business with me, and we cut a deal verbally that we later converted into writing. I would have 49 percent of the business if we were successful, and I would have the opportunity to look for another job if we were not. He told me, "If you're so sure you know the business, go prove it."

He came back with me to Toledo over Easter week, and we made a deal with First National Bank for the loans, which Bob guaranteed. I had only $20,000 that I could pledge, and that was from Susie's little trust fund. I was only making a little less than $20,000 per year at that time, so I didn't have any capital. Bob and I flew to New Jersey and gave Bekum a deposit of $100,000 dollars and secured the machines for delivery some time in July.

We had a business, and I had a deal to be president of it!

I resigned from Owens-Illinois in April 1969 after 14 years with the company.

WITH BOB EBERT ON AN ALASKA TRIP

18

On My Own and Thinking Big

Y ou wouldn't have believed the startled expressions on everyone's faces at Owens-Illinois, because people simply did not
resign from that company in those days. Ninety percent of
the people who worked for Owens-Illinois stayed there forever. While
they might not make a whole lot of money, they could live in a frater-
nal sort of organization. A clean nose and playing politics right would
earn a person security and a ticket to the good life in the corporate
world. My resigning was not only disturbing to Owens-Illinois: for
me to go into competition with them was disturbing for my father-in-
law. A retired traveler of the world, he got wind of this while he was in
Australia or New Zealand. When he came back, he barely spoke to me.
He and the chairman of Owens-Illinois were great friends, along with
a lot of other people high up in the company. They played golf, hunted,
and had warm relations over many years. He was in the social echelon
with all the top Owens-Illinois people. Biggie was a very charming guy,
although he was about to have serious health problems that eventually
took his life three or four years later.

It was 1969. I was 36, out of Owens-Illinois and on my own. I was
raising eyebrows even in the community, because in a little town like
Toledo, everybody knew everybody else—particularly in Susie's family and social strata. One of the wives of an executive of Owens-Illinois
even called me a traitor at a cocktail party. However, there was one

bit of encouragement in that period from Harris MacIntosh, president of Toledo Scale. He was married to Betty, one of the Knight family daughters. The Knight family controlled many of the banks and sat on many boards, including the board of Owens-Illinois. Mr. MacIntosh came up, put his arm around me, and said, "Frank, I can't tell you how much I admire you for your guts in going out as an entrepreneur to start your own business." He continued, "That's the way all of these businesses got founded, whether it's Owens-Illinois or Libbey Owens Ford, or Toledo Scale: Somebody had the guts to go do that. I wish you well." He was one of the top guys in the whole area, reputation-wise, and I will never forget the encouragement from a man of that stature when my own father-in-law and his friends were terribly disappointed in me. Biggie forgot his earlier advice at my wedding. "Think big, Frank," he had said.

That remained a bit of a wound for my father-in-law the rest of his life, and our relationship was never really the same. He never asked about how things were going or visited the plant. I was too busy to let that pain affect my work.

Bob Ebert had, among other interests, an advertising company in Statesville, NC named AIM Advertising, Inc. I thought it was a great name connoting goals, and directions. Susie called all around the country to see if it was available. That's how we came up with the name for AIM Packaging Company

I spent the time before the machines were delivered going after bottle business that required new molds to be built. I also had to be sure we had all the auxiliary equipment necessary for the plants: grinders, blenders, chillers, compressors, fork trucks, machine tools, box makers, all that stuff we had to acquire, including office equipment, as we started from scratch.

I hired a man named John Miller to be plant manager. He had been an Owens-Illinois employee in the Toledo development center. I knew him from the Baltimore plant when he was production manager there. We began to look for all levels of employees to run the plant, as we got ready to start up. I ran my tail off traveling, getting the customers, and getting ready for production. I was able to have the capacity almost totally loaded for those four machines by the time they arrived in late June. We went through the drill of setting them up and learning to run them and all the necessary auxiliary equipment.

Our biggest success was with Helene Curtis. I had given them back their mold money when I was with Owens-Illinois. To get their business, I essentially cut the price on Suave Shampoo bottles that were being made by a division of Eli Lily called Creative Packaging. The price was probably $70 per thousand, and I cut it to $55 per thousand making a hero of their purchasing agent, Jim Dalton, who became a good friend for life. I had the molds made in two months, and then I loaded two machines with bottle orders. We turned out excellent quality bottles in quantities of 10 to 15 million per year for Helen Curtis. Next, I sold the L. Perigo Company in Allegan, Michigan a mouthwash container. From there on, we were going in all directions to find bottle business, some through distributors who, with their sales force, could cover more territory than I could.

I was doing it all. I was president of the company, I was out selling, and I was doing the buying and an awful lot of hiring and scheduling. Bob Ebert spent a great deal of time with me to help with the manufacturing side of the business because he had been a plant manager with Rubbermaid at one time. We were able to hire Sam Carter, another Owens-Illinois employee from the accounting department. Sam came in as comptroller and eventually became a partner of mine as the saga continued. He was very helpful because he had worked in the Owens-Illinois plastic factories in Atlanta and Dallas and then had come into the financial side of the business in Toledo, Ohio. He was from Roanoke, Virginia, and was making less money than I was, so he was eager to get out and do his own thing. Sam was a very bright guy with the ability to get many things done from the financial control standpoint. He had good judgment on many levels of factory management as well. He worked very hard and was instrumental in our success. We remain good friends.

Before we got Sam on board, Kathleen Harkness was the administrative manager. She was a lovely old biddy who was somewhat bumbling but meticulous and loyal. She would come to work at eight in the morning and stay until eight at night and then drive an hour and a half home south of Toledo. Kathleen was overworked and not a good secretary who could take dictation, type well and handle the telephone. So I put the word out that I was looking for an experienced secretary. Fortunately I got a great one when I hired Gerry Behm. Gerry did everything with a charming voice and manner. She was very attractive, very bright and was always projected a good mood. Customers loved her as did the other employees. She was my secretary for 20 years and we've stayed in touch since then.

Ours was a down-to-earth, scratching kind of business as we hired hourly employees to operate this 24/7 operation with three shifts. Near our plant in Port Clinton, Ohio, we had bedrooms and a shower, where Bob Ebert and I would often stay because we had to take care of business. My home was 30 miles away in Perrysburg. We couldn't work any more hours because there were no more in the day. I'll never forget the first railcar load we ever shipped—quart plastic bottles for kerosene-based lamp oil—to the Kansas City area, and I personally helped load the first railcar. Our humble but hard-working beginnings meant everybody did whatever necessary to get it done. One night, Bob Ebert was working late on one of the second or third shifts. He was taking a break sitting in the men's restrooms with his legs showing down below the stall. Don Kelly, the supervisor of the plant, came in there and screamed at him, "Get your ass out there on the line! We've got trouble on machine number four!" Bob said, "I'll be right out!" Kelly didn't know he was talking to the owner. It was a funny thing that nobody had any special rank. We had a job to do, and there were no extra people to do it.

The travails of finding and keeping good people, sorting out the bad ones, making sure the product was as good as we could make it, and getting more business was a great experience for me. But the result was, by the time we got those four machines up and running, we ordered four more because business was pouring in. Customers were coming to us because they had heard that not only did we make good bottles, we also made them at a good price and on time. The price wars were beginning to heat up in the industry. Owens-Illinois had always tried to control the prices in glass bottles. With their capacity and 12 plastic bottle plants scattered around the country, they could do a great deal of that.

By October of 1969, having just started the operation in July, we turned a profit! It was an exciting time for bankers and a very exciting time for me. I had a car, a salary of $25,000, health insurance, and life insurance. Business was going along great. Bob Ebert was very happy; I was very happy. Our plant was struggling to keep up with demand. We were building molds fast and furiously. By the time we had the eighth machine loaded, I knew that I was running out of me. I needed some help taking care of the customers and running the business. I had joined the Society of the Plastics Industry, Plastic Bottle Division. The president of the society was George Babcock of Owens-Illinois. By that time, the Owens-Illinois people were being much friendlier to me. They had gotten over the shock of my leaving, so they urged me to join the society, and I did.

Success helps forgiveness. Failure simply confirms a loser. Besides, I was buying most of our corrugated boxes from OI and was a good customer. Bill Laimbeer, the OI General Manager of Paper Products Division, became a good friend and still is today.

WITH BILL LAIMBEER AT THE GRAND HOTEL,
MACKINAC ISLAND, MICHIGAN

19

Blasting Off

Of the first four machines, I had filled up the two bigger ones with business. Soon, we also filled up the two smaller ones. We had two Bekum 220s for making bigger bottles and two Bekum 110s for smaller bottles. I was able to get all of the business of the Richardson Merrill Company in Cincinnati for Cepacol mouthwash sample bottles. We produced around 10 million four-ounce bottles per year on those machines, working them 24 hours a day, seven days a week.

Jim Asbeck worked for BF Goodrich which produced the resin that we used for Cepacol bottles. I knew him when he was calling on Owens-Illinois, and we got to be friends. I realized we needed a facility in the east, because shipping empty plastic bottles was too costly from the Midwest. I hired Jim Asbeck to be the general manager of the plant that we bought from Continental Oil, with four similar Bekum machines in West Springfield, Massachusetts. The company had been called Vinyl-Made. They were not successful, so we were able to buy the machines and the plant at that location very reasonably.

I thought Jim knew a great deal about the business. He talked a good line, was a big company BS-er. And he never got an order for bottles in the two years that he worked for me. He was a very attractive guy with a very pretty wife, and he played a nice game of golf. That's part of the vagaries and vicissitudes of any business. You pick people, hoping that they're going to turn out well. He never got one order! He had me come in and help him, and we did get Clairol Shampoo bottle business and other business at Colgate that I had already lined up. We were able to produce the bottle orders in the eastern area near where they filled them, but we had to struggle to get business there, and Jim didn't last very long. He actually tried to go into business for himself and was talking about buying machines while he was on my payroll.

AIM PACKAGING, INC.

For Industrial Park, P. O. Box 278, Port Clinton, Ohio 43452 Phone: 419-732-2139

July 23, 1969

Mr. & Mrs. W. L. Harris
South Aspen Street
Lincolnton, North Carolina

Dear Mom & Dad:

How do you like the stationery of our new company?

I've intended to write or call the last month or six weeks but as I'm certain you realize there is just not enough hours in the day to do all the things I want to do and should do. With that excuse hopefully acceptable, I'll go on to the reports.

Our business is coming along extremely well with the sale of many millions of containers and the commencement of production on our machines which began to arrive on the 12th of June. We really have done an amazing job of getting started as quickly as we have with all the complex electrically, hydraulic, pneumatic and other systems required for blow molding. Separately, I'm sending you a sample of our first bottle which we produced in early July. It may not be beautiful to anyone else but it certainly is to us.

I've had to be less of a business monk than I expected I might be in starting this new company. Susie and I have maintained a reasonable amount of social activity and golf to keep things in balance. We are leaving this week for a week-end in Leland, Michigan with Bill and Ann Lathrop and Bob Ebert will be here to keep the store.

I hope you can plan to come up to visit us this fall and see the operation.

Dad, I trust know news is good news concerning your health and that you are progressing rapidly back to full strength and speed. Will you be able to make the trip to Ohio this fall?

LETTER TO MY PARENTS DURING THE FOUNDING OF
AIM PACKAGING (CONTINUED NEXT PAGE)

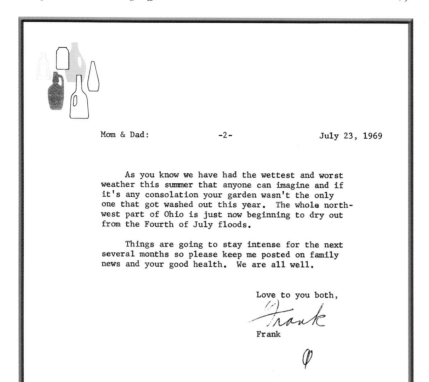

Mom & Dad: -2-   July 23, 1969

As you know we have had the wettest and worst weather this summer that anyone can imagine and if it's any consolation your garden wasn't the only one that got washed out this year. The whole northwest part of Ohio is just now beginning to dry out from the Fourth of July floods.

Things are going to stay intense for the next several months so please keep me posted on family news and your good health. We are all well.

Love to you both,

Frank

h

He ultimately went to work for Bob Kittridge of the Fabrical Company, a competitor. Bob Kittridge kept him around for about a year, and then he also fired him. We both made a very bad judgment call with Jim Asbeck. Hopefully he found a measure of success in a different field.

We were roaring along, business was good, and we were making lots of money. I love to say that one year after we had the machines installed in the first plant, I had gone from making $20,000 a year at Owens-Illinois to making $20,000 a month at AIM Packaging. We had nice new cars and things of that sort. We took great trips to play golf and shoot birds when we eventually were able to slack off little bit. From the start-up of AIM Packaging, it felt like we worked 24 hours a day.

After AIM Packaging made me more financially able, I joined the
Erie Marsh Club—a duck hunting club that dates back to the 1870s—
just across the line from Toledo in Michigan. Many prominent bank
presidents and major industry people from around that part of Ohio,
particularly Toledo, belonged to it. They had separate cottages where
we'd stay and guides who would take us out to the blinds if we needed
them. The marsh was about 1,000 acres, and it was absolutely wonderful. Susie and I would take our son, Walter, when he got old enough to
shoot. We had a fabulous time shooting the plentiful ducks and geese.
The camaraderie with other members during the early morning break-
fasts and after the shooting was great fun. Membership at Erie Marsh
was special. Susie was a pretty good shot and would pop one every
now and then from a very surprising long distance that I thought out
of range. She'd take a poke at a bird, and it would drop out of the sky.
She would be thrilled and I was thrilled too.

SON WALTER AFTER A DUCK HUNT AT OUR LODGE

HEADING TO THE DUCK BLIND WITH MY DOG

Since the club rules only allowed me to bring one guest to Erie Marsh, I decided what I needed was my own duck hunting club. After a while, I was able to lease a marsh along Lake Erie and maintained it for about 20 years. That was where we shot when we weren't shooting at Erie Marsh Club. At my marsh, I sometimes brought as many as 20 people. We had six blinds scattered around 130 acres of the marsh and a big hunting lodge with a captain, Glen Smith, who took care of the lodge and fishing boat. Opening day of duck season, people would fly in from all over the United States and stay at the lodge and be entertained with big, fancy dinners. We were always out the next morning by 7 a.m. for shooting in the blinds. By 10:00 we were back at the lodge preparing to go to Rockwell Trout Club for lunch and fishing for trout. Then back to the lodge for a big dinner in the evening.

For about five years in a row, I had A. Gary Shilling—an economist of considerable note—come and speak at my lodge. He would come out from New York and give us an economic speech so that it was as legal as you could make it for the IRS. We would also have plant tours of our bottle factory, which was in the area. Bill Stokely of the Stokely-Van Camp Company, which owned the Gatorade brand at that time, became a good friend. He would say, "Well, guess we have to do the obligatory plant tour again." So I'd take them through the bottle factory where I had about a half a million square feet of space with 700 employees. Entertaining customers with hunting, fishing, and golf, all tied in beautifully. I used to say I sold more bottles in a duck blind and on a golf course than I ever did sitting across the table with customers in their offices.

One time the director of purchasing for Colgate, Al Storer, flew into Toledo on the Monsanto Plane. Monsanto was my biggest competitor in the plastic bottle business. We had dinner that night at the hunting lodge and got up the next morning and shot our limit of ducks by 8:30 a.m. We then drove about 20 miles to Rockwell Trout Club and caught our limit of trout. Finally we went to Belmont Country Club, where we had lunch and played 18 holes of golf. At the end of the day, I took him to the Toledo airport and deposited him in front of the Monsanto airplane to fly to St. Louis, where he was being entertained the next day by my biggest competitor. Al Storer loved the good

GROUSE HUNTING WITH SUSIE, CIRCA 1966

WITH BILL STOKELY, CEO OF STOKELY-VAN CAMP
AFTER A PRODUCTIVE DUCK HUNT

life, and I loved guys like him who loved to be entertained, because it was a great way to do business. We were probably doing $5 million worth of bottle business every year with Colgate for shampoos and mouthwashes.

That part of the old business world has mostly dried up. You can't entertain anybody anymore. You can't give them any gifts. We had an awfully good time hunting and fishing and going to dinners and theatre. It was very hard, however, to do anything better than the competitors, because everybody else did it too.

After joining the Society of the Plastics Industry (SPI), at the urging of some Owens-Illinois people and others (including Jim Asbeck), I went to the first meeting in New York City. I observed that the president of the Bottle Division of SPI at that time worked for a relatively small company, Kerr Glass, which had been part of Armstrong World

Industries. Its general sales manager was Arthur R. McCamey, a tall, good-looking West Virginia graduate and Marine veteran who had a great deal of poise. I heard from key people in the industry that he was a good operator. I had run myself ragged trying to cover all the bases and also have a normal life, so I wondered if McCamey would be interested in coming to Port Clinton, Ohio, and working for AIM Packaging. We were the dazzling new boy on the street in the industry, getting business and getting high marks for quality and service. I was able to develop molds to make the bottles in four or six weeks, while Owens-Illinois took four to six months, as did many of the big competitors. I was able to do that because I flat knew what was required and how to get it done fast and correctly with mold makers in Canada and other places. Customers loved us. I asked Art if he would consider coming to work for AIM Packaging.

Art was cautious, but he came to Toledo with his family to look over the area and stayed with us at our hunting/fishing lodge that we rented along Lake Erie. Ann McCamey and Susie had met earlier at another SPI meeting in Bermuda, and got to know each other better. Art and Ann brought their kids along, and we had a big cook-out along the beach on a beautiful summer evening in July of 1971. Art and I were talking about AIM Packaging and my need for more help to increase the business, when he said, "I'd like to see your factory." The plant was five miles away. We hopped in my car and went to the plant about 10 or 11 at night. There were eight machines running at absolute top speed spitting out bottles of all shapes and sizes and colors. He was in absolute awe of what he saw, compared with the slow process of the machines that they had at Kerr. I was kicking their tail pretty well, as well as just about all the old line glass companies which had tried to be plastic bottle producers and use their past reputation to get business.

The visit with Art went well so I arranged for him to meet with Bob Ebert. We had a golf game at Belmont Country Club and were able to cut a deal. We paid him $40,000 a year plus a brand new Mercury Marquis. Now I had Art McCamey as general manager of the Midwest operation and Jim Asbeck general manager of the Eastern operation. After Asbeck was gone, we found another young man who had been with Continental Cans Plastics Division named Peter Mahr. He became general manager of the Eastern operation, replacing Asbeck. He was a real hot shot for quite a while. We had good growth and good business with the team of Harris, McCamey, and Mahr in place.

I was the president doing whatever I had to do. It was a team operation.

THE CESSNA 421 OWNED BY AIM PACKAGING COMPANY. IT MADE LIFE MORE EFFICIENT AND FUN. WE USED IT EXTENSIVELY IN THE '80S

L-R, ART & ANN MCCAMEY, SAM & BETTY CARTER, SUSIE

20

The Oil Embargo and the FDA Take a Bite

N ow we switch from the good times to the bad times. After starting off like a rocket and lighting up the skies with good business and good relations, we ran into a terrible situation when the oil embargo of the mid-1970s hit, creating a feed stock supply shortage for plastics. It was very challenging whether we could get enough raw materials to run the factories and make bottles as we did not have equipment that would run alternate materials like polyethylene. We were strictly PVC clear plastic bottle producers, and it was a real shock to us and to our supplier: we were buying our raw material from Occidental Chemical, and they were struggling to get enough raw materials to supply us.

About that time, as happens with a fast-growing, emerging industry, some people in the conglomerate building business contacted us to see if we'd like to sell the company. U.S. Industries was one of them, and I had an engaging conversation with an attractive person who was looking for businesses to buy. At that time, U.S. Industries had acquired 99 different companies, and was a real hot shot on the New York Stock Exchange. Its stock was going for about $30 per share. As we held negotiations, I was operating somewhat out of fear because of the oil embargo and the debts that we still had from growing so fast and acquiring plants and machines. Also, I was burning out from all the stress from the rapid growth.

At that time we were looking at the possibility of building another factory in Kentucky to provide plastic bottles for the bourbon industry. AIM made the first plastic liquor bottles ever made in the United States, except for a few that had been made by Owens-Illinois when I was there. That was one of the markets that we believed would be emerging from glass bottles. Already we were making bottles for Old Crow bourbon, a National Distillers brand, and several others, including American Distillers and Barton Brands—half-pints and pints for bourbon, primarily, but also for clear gin liquors and vodkas. We had molds in the works for Seagram.

Conversations commenced with U.S. Industries (USI) about the growth opportunities of AIM. Their president came to see me, we had several discussions; USI came up with an offer for several million dollars, of which I would get half and also have the debt removed and the personal obligations gone. As they said, "You will now have a bigger and better bank with encouragement to develop your business better and provide the opportunities for the McCameys and the Carters and the Mahrs, your key people, and all the others working hard for opportunities from growth."

I went to Bob Ebert and told him we ought to sell the business. I had never had any money of any appreciable amount, and a couple million dollars was a hell of a lot of money back in those days. The vagaries of the marketplace and the oil situation in the Middle East were very scary to me then. Bob did not want to sell because he had more resources with which to be risk tolerant than I did. But I said, "Look, I'll make it real easy. I'll sell my half of it to you for the same price, and I'll work for you." For whatever reason, he decided not to do that. He took his money, and I took my money, and we parted best of friends, as we've remained all these years since selling AIM Packaging in 1972.

I then became a millionaire-plus before I was 40. I had lots of reasons to be terribly enthusiastic about our new owner, who would provide us with the capital to grow and prosper further without the personal risk. I was riding pretty high with all the top management at U.S. Industries as we met financial objectives. Over the next few years, I had offers to be group vice president and run half a dozen USI plastic operations—everything from plastic bags to plastic materials for irrigation and pipe and automotive, which I gratefully declined. I didn't want to start chasing myself traveling again for a big company. I stayed on with the two plants that we had in Massachusetts and Ohio. We never did build the plant in Kentucky because of an FDA ruling that cancer might be caused by unpolymerized vinylchloride monomer, the building block for polyvinylchloride. A few molecules had been found in liquor that was packaged in PVC, and PVC bottles were banned. We got stuck with a big cost of inventory that customers would not buy. That market died instantly.

So there were two heavy hits—one, the oil embargo, and, two, the FDA ruling, which I'm sure to this day was engineered by the Glass Container Manufacturers Institute (GCMI) trying to find something wrong with plastic. It was an absurd allegation because plastic of that particular type was used for everything from packaging cheese to baby formula and arterial replacement, and it's still being used in huge volumes for those applications. But that's war in the industrial world. A company that can't win on the merits of its product, glass bottles in this instance, will attempt to find fault with the competition.

21

When the Going Gets Tough . . .

In 1975, a severe recession took place in the automobile supply business, the furniture business, and the textile business, of which U.S. Industries had probably 60 to 70 percent of its total dollar volume in sales—about $2 billion overall. That same year, we did very well and turned in about 10 percent of the total profits of USI when we were only doing about $15 million to $16 million in annual sales. Because of USI's bank loan covenants from all the borrowings they'd done for companies they'd bought, they had to declare a moratorium on paying any bonuses. That left Art McCamey, Sam Carter, Peter Mahr, and me without any of the bonuses, which would have been a good 30 to 40 percent more of pay. As you can imagine, I was very disappointed that this money was not forthcoming under the contract we had. It was superseded by the contracts they had with their bank loans.

After gnashing our teeth for a year or more and trying to figure out if we were going to come out of this all right, McCamey and the other key people were talking about quitting because they had not been rewarded as they had been promised. I went to Gordon Walker, the group vice president of USI, who had become a friend as I sat on the executive committee for his particular segment of the business. I told him I wanted to buy the business back. We had a lot of discussion along those lines, and he told me he did not want to sell it. But after many tries, I was finally able to persuade him to sell it back to us for just a little over what we had been paid for it when USI bought AIM years before.

Bob Ebert was gone. His capital resources were not available as he chose not to get back into that business due to his many other investments. He was always, and still is, a friend. But I think he could see that bottles were a potential commodity, meaning that the quality would be the same from all producers and the only way to compete would be on price, which would be driven down. The good days, he figured, could be drawing to a close. Whatever his motivations were, he declined to get back into it with the capital we needed.

I went on a search to find the money, reluctant to put my own capital back into it. I had read how most entrepreneurs lose most of their wealth when they keep trying to get richer. My reputation around Toledo had been superb as a businessman and entrepreneur, and I was riding pretty high. One of my neighbors, with whom I hunted and played paddle tennis, Hans Jones, was president of the Commodore Perry Company. The company consisted of two hotels, an industrial park, 20 percent of Ohio Citizens Bank, a portfolio of $6 million to $8 million dollars in stock, and a smattering of other good businesses. He was a Stanford business school graduate MBA and a very attractive guy with an extremely attractive wife.

I talked with him and his board members. After almost too much time passed and USI was about to walk away from the deal, we were finally able to put it together. Sam, Art, and I would be 50 percent owners. We were able to buy AIM Packaging back from USI for about a million and a half dollars more than they had paid us for it several years before. We had grown significantly and we needed the capital to grow further.

As an aside, I was so upset with USI over the bonus issue that I secretly went to the Owens-Illinois general manager of the Plastics Products Division, Bill Graham, whom I had reported to at one time years before, and persuaded him to sell me their eight Bekum machines. Owens-Illinois had dropped out of that business after the problems of PVC with the FDA, and the machines were sitting, disassembled, in a New Jersey plant. They were exactly the same type we had. Owens-

Illinois eventually bought them in defense, to compete, because their own designed machines did not work. I was able to buy those machines and a lot of auxiliary equipment for a very low price, around $300,000 to $400,000 for what would have been $3 million to $4 million worth of equipment when they were new. They were in pretty poor shape, but they were reparable. I started a new company called C&M (Carter & McCamey) Plastics and moved it into another factory site in the Erie Industrial Park in Port Clinton. McCamey and Carter were going to run that operation while I was under the restriction of a covenant not to compete with U.S. Industries for five years.

22

The Final Lap

So here we go again with new partners, board meetings, plant visits, and teaching them the business. The new board of eight had four representatives from each 'side.' They were represented by the chairman of the board of Libbey Owens Ford, Don McCone; Bill Webb, the chairman and CEO of Ohio Citizens Bank (the second largest bank in Toledo); his brother, Tom Webb, a lawyer; and Hans Jones. Our side was represented by Art McCamey, Frank Harris, Sam Carter, and Jim Kline as our legal representative.

Thinking of Jim Kline reminds me I should mention the great lawyers I've had the pleasure of working with through the years. Greg Alexander was a lawyer with the firm of Shumaker, Loop and Kendrick and had been a friend from my earliest days in Toledo before either of us was married. He handled the closing of the first house we owned in Maumee and was very encouraging when I considered starting my own business. He said, "Go do it. You have the confidence to be successful." Naturally Greg became the "incorporator" of AIM and legal counsel. He served on the first board of directors along with Bob Ebert, Paul Shumaker, a Dutch friend of Bob's from Deventer, Netherlands and myself. Shumaker, a very interesting chap, was a powerful businessman with plastic plants in several European countries.

Greg Alexander is married to Connie Urschel whose family had a large limestone quarry. Greg eventually left the law firm to join the

family business. I then chose James F. White as the replacement lawyer. Jim was a super bright young man with degrees from Princeton,
Wharton, NYU and Ohio State. He has represented us well through
some very tough times as well as good ones. When we began the
attempted buy out of the Commodore Perry Company Jim sent us
to another legal firm because of a conflict of interest. His firm represented Ohio Citizens Bank, which was controlled by the Commodore
Perry Company and would have been part of the buyout. The firm Jim
recommended was Eastman and Smith, where Jim Kline became our
lawyer as well as a board member of AIM. Jim Kline served us well
in our dealings with the Commodore Perry Company and with the

THE TWO
SIDES OF
MY GOOD
FRIEND
JIM WHITE.
"ON THE
OTHER
HAND!"

L-R, JIM & SUE WHITE, FRANK & SUSIE HARRIS, LARRY & MARTY
SELHORST, JAN & MILLER MYERS. A WONDERFUL PARTY FOR MY 70TH
BIRTHDAY (AND ALSO LARRY'S) AT LA PLAYA CLUB GIVEN BY GOOD
FRIENDS JIM & SUE WHITE AND MILLER & JAN MYERS. THERE WERE
70–80 PEOPLE ATTENDING WITH ART MCCAMEY AND BOB SMITH
"ROASTING" ME AND BILL GUNTON AND OTHERS ROASTING LARRY.

Green Cove/Wild Wings Development. Eventually Jim left us when
he became general counsel for Cooper tire.

All these lawyers remain good friends, especially Jim White and
his lovely wife, Sue. Susie and I have enjoyed traveling with Jim and
Sue socially and on golf and hunting trips. Jim White is a very special
man.

Now at this stage in the continuing saga of AIM Packaging, we had
raised the capital through the Commodore Perry Company. We had
two plants plus a third in the Erie Industrial Park in a building that was
about three quarters of a million square feet and far better than the first
one. It gave us a lot of room to expand the business. Away we went
with a new financial partner, and things were going great again. C&M
Plastics merged into AIM. I was CEO; Carter & McCamey were executive VPs of administration and operations, respectively. The three of

us held equal shares of 50 percent of the new AIM. We did this with no personal capital and no risk, except our time and talents. The team was together again. The business was good. The shortages that we worried about had passed. The oil embargo had passed, and we were doing just swimmingly.

Then about 1978, polyethylene terephthalate or PET was developed for big beverage bottles, water bottles, and many other products. It was a beautiful new clear material that required very expensive new, high speed production machines and we hoped to get into that business. But the Commodore Perry Company and its family owners, most of whom were old, decided that they wanted to sell all their businesses, and they were not in the mood to invest anything further in any company.

The response of the AIM Packaging team, including Hans Jones, was an attempt to buy the entire Commodore Perry Company. We bid something like $20 million with backing from several banks that would have liked to have had control of the Ohio Citizens Bank, which was part of that deal. It turned out that Bill Webb's son, Willard Webb IV, and his wife, who were investment bankers in New York City, came in with a bid of $1 more per share than we bid. After agonizing efforts trying to get them to work with us, the family voted to take the money and not worry about Frank Harris, his partners, or about Hans Jones. Hans was having a fight with the other members of his family and the Webbs.

We had, then, a total leverage buyout of the Commodore Perry Company, which included the 50 percent control of AIM Packaging by Willard Webb IV and his wife, Susan. She was a former banker with Manufacturers Hanover Trust and dealing with her was like dealing with the wicked witch of all time. We found ourselves in another situation where our new partners had no money to allow us to expand. Our business was very good, but we lost employees because we couldn't grow with the new technology of PET that eventually replaced most PVC as the preferred plastic for packaging.

We had more orders than we could produce with our existing manufacturing capacity, and had just gotten a contract to make all the Windex bottles in the USA from the Drackett Company.

So, while I had restrictions to not spend more than $25,000 without board approval, which was stalemated by the Webb side, I learned that Fabrical, our competitor with plants in Summerville, New Jersey, and Santa Ana, California, was for sale. I knew Bob Kitteridge, its owner, and was able to cut a deal to buy the business for about a million and lease the plants for $25,000 per month until I could work out the buy-out of the hostile Webbs.

We got the added capacity we needed, but the Webbs were not happy as they wanted and needed the cash to pay their bank debts! It was absolutely impossible to deal with the Webbs who were financial types. We had very bad relations from day one, first of all because we lost the bid to them, and secondly, because they thought we were being paid too much. We had board meetings in which we nearly came to blows. It seemed the only way out was to buy the business back again—buy their 50 percent share.

After months and months of fighting and trying to figure out how to do that, I was able to come up with support from our material supplier, Occidental Chemical, to get six month terms for the raw material that we bought. That generated $3 million of working capital that we could then use along with bank loans of $3 million to buy the Commodore Perry's 50 percent interest in AIM Packaging.

We did that, and 1980 turned out to be the worst time we could imagine. The bank loans went to 22 percent interest. For the next three years, we were bailing as hard as we could just to keep the business afloat with the bank debt we had and the scheduled retirement of the special terms with Occidental Chemical. Timing is everything, good and bad.

Susie and I were invited to view the 1983 America's Cup Races at Newport, Rhode Island, on a big yacht chartered by Occidental Chemical's Russ Gervais, the general manager of the Resin Division. While there, he announced to me that Occidental Chemical had just fired him. I said, "Russ, you've helped save this corporation, and you're as sharp a guy as I know. It may be time for you to think about running a smaller company. Would you like to discuss running AIM Packaging?" Under those stressful times, I was once again ready to get out of a deal. I had enough money to do it, but Carter and McCamey did not, and they had their names on some paper too that could have hurt them seriously if the company went belly up.

RUSS GERVAIS AND HIS WIFE AT THE AMERICA'S CUP
RACE 1984. I ASKED HIM TO CONSIDER WORKING FOR
ME AT AIM AND THEN MADE HIM PRESIDENT.

About that same time, Art McCamey came into my office after having had a biopsy on a mole on his abdomen. He announced that he had phase four melanoma skin cancer. The worst is phase five. The prognosis for survival was very poor. I'll never forget that great big guy with tears in his eyes, saying, "I'm not handling this very well." I'm not sure who could handle it very well.

That surgery put Art out of business for almost a year. He survived the terrible operations of removing the lymph nodes in his groin and armpit and removing a big sausage chunk out of his abdomen. He was on pins and needles for many years. Blessedly, he survived and remains

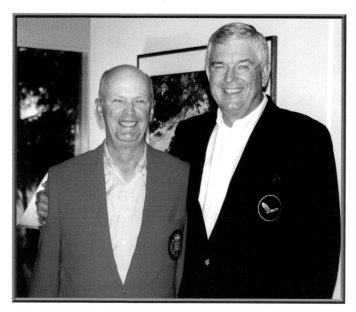

WITH BUSINESS PARTNER ART MCCAMEY LONG
AFTER WE SOLD AIM PACKAGING

GREAT
FRIENDS ART
AND ANNE
MCCAMEY.
ART WAS
A TOAST/
ROAST
SPEAKER AT
MY 70TH
BIRTHDAY
PARTY.

a dear friend. I brought Russ Gervais in to be the president of AIM
Packaging, and I moved up to Chairman. I got out of the way and let
him do what had to be done, which he did extremely well. He was able
to get rid of all the "old Charleys" that are typical in a corporation
where they've helped you in the critical times but they weren't doing
the job any more. He brought in new people. He brought in a lot of
new things, and he also cleaned up the quality that had slipped as we
had become too big, too sloppy, or too distracted.

We made progress burning off the debt, but it was still too steep.
About that time the prices of bottles in the industry began to tumble.
Competition was brutal. We had the Imco Division. We had the Sewell
Company. We had Owens-Illinois, Continental Can, American Can,
and Monsanto, all cutting prices as we all raced to oblivion. The industry was mature, and it was now scrambling for bottle business to load
on the machines, because these machines cost from $150 to $500 an hour
whether you ran them or not. We needed to convert plastic into bottles
and then into cash. The industry was very, very tough, yet we were still
one of the best in the business. We still made some very attractive profit
margins, even though they were being eaten up by our debt.

As the AIM Packaging saga went on we were contacted by Metal
Box Industries of England to acquire our company. They were heavily
involved in the toiletry and cosmetics business in the east, manufacturing other containers, closures, fitments, and boxes for powder and
cosmetics. When their general manager from England visited me, we
got very close to negotiating their buying us out. That discussion happened about the same time that two guys, formerly from Continental
Can, Ed Horrigan and Phil Silver, started a new company called Silgan.
They had gone with Morgan Stanley and raised enough capital to buy
Monsanto's $100 million bottle business and Amaco's $150 million bottle business. They bought three or four other companies, and they were
on the move with big, deep pockets. We were looking to be bought by
Metal Box, when Metal Box got involved with buying Carnaud, the
largest can company in Europe. Metal Box called us to say that the
digestion period from buying Carnaud would take a year or two. Then
perhaps they would be interested in AIM Packaging again.

It was 1988, and I was into land development while still being Chairman of AIM. AIM was facing the dilemma of needing to upgrade its bottle making equipment but without capital or borrowing capacity. We were still burning off big debts. So I called Ed Horrigan of Silgan and told him the situation and asked if he was interested in buying AIM Packaging. He said yes, it would be a perfect fit. We sold the business to Silgan in 1989, and our man Russ Gervais went along with them to be its president. Art McCamey, Sam Carter and I took our several millions from that sale and retired from the bottle business. McCamey never went back into any business except for investments. Carter got into the home building business. We're all retired now, and we're still very good friends and stay in touch with each other, particularly McCamey, who has homes in Harbor Springs, Michigan, and Harbor Ridge, Florida. He has been the president of Harbor Ridge and is very popular everywhere. Sam and Betty Carter are constantly moving from place to place, which makes at least one of them happy.

L-R SAM CARTER, FRANK HARRIS, ART MCCAMEY

AIM Packaging—from 1969 to 1989—was the major thrust of my efforts, and those were the players I shared it with. We were also great entertainers of customers when that was something that you could do at golf and fishing and theater, and we made a lot of good friends that are still in touch, at least those who are still alive, from those industries we served.

Geneva Business Services, Inc.
A Geneva Company
5 Park Plaza
Irvine, California 92714
Facsimile: 714-756-0573
Telex: 469386 GENEVA SNA
(714) 756-2200 (800) 854-4643

GENEVA

March 3, 1989

Frank Harris
227 Polynesia Court
Marco Island, FL 33937

Dear Frank:

The vision that created AIM Packaging was still the driving force that kept this deal on course. You possess a foresight into a buyer's mind that I thought only dealmakers like myself were supposed to have. I found your instincts to be uncanny and accurate.

It is no wonder that you have been successful not only in your development of AIM but in your real estate ventures as well. I hope that someday our paths will once more cross. Whether its a personal situation of yours or a business associates, I would like to work with you again.

In the meantime, may your golf scores continue to improve now that the weight of these past months have been eased from your shoulders. Thank you again for allowing myself and Geneva the opportunity to assist you.

Respectfully,

A. John Dorey
Vice President - Managing Director
Mergers & Acquisitions

AJD:rb

LETTER FROM JOHN DOREY WHO HELPED ME SELL
AIM PACKAGING FOR THE LAST TIME

Dear Frank & Susie,

Thank you for the generous check & I certainly appreciate the kind words. I, too, have enjoyed our friendship & working relationship over the many years. All of you are very special to us & we appreciate your sincerity... our sons think you're the greatest! Bryan will never forget the fishing trip with Walter & he still talks about the trip & BMW ride. Frank, I consider the working experience invaluable. A Big "Thank You" for everything.

As ever, Gerry

NOTE FROM GERRY BEHM, MY SECRETARY FOR 20 YEARS, WHOM I GAVE A BONUS OF $25,000 WHEN I SOLD THE COMPANY. SHE STAYED ON FOR ANOTHER 15 YEARS WITH SILGAN, THE BUYER OF AIM PACKAGING, INC.

23

Helping Others Help Themselves

I t gives a person great pleasure to help someone succeed in life. It gives even greater pleasure to have them acknowledge that without the help, success wouldn't have been possible.

About 1977 or 1978, a personable young man named Michael Brinker ran a men's clothing store in Perrysburg, Ohio. He had been an assistant golf pro at one time but his business was not doing well in this little suburb of Toledo. I was talking with him one day, and he said he was afraid he was going to have to close his shop and go back to work as an assistant golf pro. I told him that I didn't think there was a hell of a lot of potential for assistant golf pros. There are myriad of those out there already.

I said. "Mike, that's not the way to go. Maybe your location is wrong. Where do you need to be?"

"I need to be in downtown Toledo, but I don't have any money."

We worked out a business plan and I made arrangements for bank financing. I structured a situation where I had 51 percent of the business until the bank loan got paid off. I don't recall putting any cash into it. I just had a net worth that allowed me to guarantee the bank loan.

Brinker found a place in Toledo and set up shop. He grew so quickly that he has since moved into a bigger place. He acquired a line of the best clothing available for lawyers and executives operating out of downtown Toledo. He has done very well for himself.

He paid off the bank. I brought in some accounting people for him and then I let him buy me out for a fairly nominal sum, around $100,000. His business is now doing $1 million to $1.5 million per year.

The other part of our deal was that I could buy my clothes and my son's clothes at cost, plus 10 percent. There is a 100 percent markup on clothes. My son has moved away, but we still get a suit for him every now and then.

Now that I am in Florida and don't need them anymore, I have given away all but two or three of the suits. I kept a dark blue one for funerals. I have about 40 sport coats. It's a nice little perk. That's an interesting story that worked out very well. Michael Brinker is a great young man although, like the rest of us, he's not so young anymore.

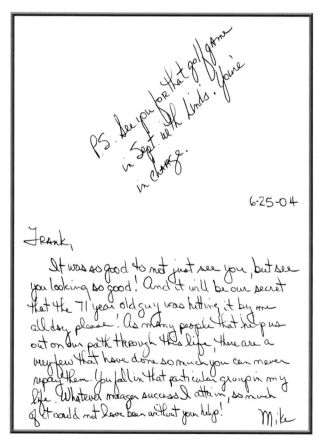

LETTER FROM MIKE BRINKER

24

Country Club Champion

Nineteen seventy-seven was a great year. I won my first country club championship at the Belmont Country Club in Toledo. I beat Ashel Bryant, the chairman of the board of one of the biggest banks in town. Ashel was in his early 60s, and I was in my early 40s. It was a 36-hole match play tournament in one day—36 holes after you had won in match play and eliminated the rest of the field over several weeks. It was down to the two of us.

It was quite an event because I always hit the ball a long way, and Ashel didn't hit it very far at all. But he hit it so very straight. I remember thinking to myself, "This old crock is hitting that ball closer with a 4-wood than I am with a 7-iron." It was driving me crazy. I had been up three or four holes on him on the first 18 and thought I had everything going my way. All of a sudden, he started knocking balls close to the pin. And I started missing greens. We were all even when we got to the 36th hole. I pulled my drive into a creek bed, but somehow I hit the ball out. I then knocked it over the green, chipped it back on and made a 5. Ashel was right down the middle with two short of the green, and then he missed the chip of around 60 yards and made a 5, so we were tied going into the 37th hole.

There were 40 or 50 people watching us. My wife and daughter were there, before Gingi drove back to Skidmore College in Saratoga Springs, New York. We went to the extra hole, Number one, a par 4. I hit my drive into the sand bunker on the first fairway. He hit his drive right down the middle. His next shot was onto the green. Ashel played first because the sand bunker where I had hit my shot was quite a bit farther than he had hit his drive. Somehow I was able to get a 3-iron out of the sand trap and onto the green. I was farther away from the hole than he was, but I was able to sink about a 30-foot birdie putt, and he missed his 15-foot putt. And that was the end of the match!

It was my first absolutely thrilling experience in competitive golf, and I still talk with Ashel about it. He's a delightful guy, almost 90 years old now, and he said, "I wake up thinking about that match often." His son also said he still talks about that match.

I was so cranked up that I barely slept the night after I won. It was just a wonderful, exhilarating experience. My wife and daughter were excited too—but also glad the 10-hour match was over.

25

Pine Valley

I have played golf with many big shots in my day—vice presidents of Owens Corning, Michael Jordan, Neil Armstrong—and at the most prestigious golf clubs around the world. But I consider one of my greatest golf achievements to be my membership at Pine Valley Golf Club in Pine Valley, New Jersey the number 1 ranked golf club in the world. It's a devilishly challenging course too.

Ben Boyd, executive VP of Owens-Corning, was a very good golfer and a member of Toledo Country Club and Pine Valley. I was invited several times to go with him to Pine Valley to play and help him entertain customers. One of the absolute best things that ever happened to me was on the fourth hole at Pine Valley.

Pine Valley was run by a "dictator" named John Arthur Brown, who was the president for 50 years. Mr. Brown was in his late 80s, a tall, imposing man with piercing eyes. He was sitting on his green golf cart in his green jacket next to the club house at the fourth hole, a par four, which comes back to the club house. I hit my second shot about two feet from the pin and tapped in the putt.

As I walked off the green, Mr. Brown stood up and asked, "Was that a birdie?"

I said, "Yes, sir, it was."

Ben Boyd, my host, said, "Mr. Brown, this is Frank Harris. I've had him down here as a guest several times, and he's a pretty good golfer.

He absolutely loves Pine Valley, and he expressed an interest in being a member."

There was a terrible pause from this old man with his piercing eyes. He looked at me for several seconds and I felt my spine begin to melt.

Finally, he said, "Well, he looks like the kind of young person we ought to have in here. Get his paperwork done." So I had to scramble and find another five members to write a letter on my behalf.

In six months, I became a member of Pine Valley, which I regard as one of the greatest things that ever happened to me in golf and in life. I have been a member since 1973. I have some 40 trophy plates, which have pictures of Pine Valley holes on them. I won a lot of events—I should say flights in the events. I have never been good enough to play against the very best players who belong there, though I have played with them. Some of those great golf members were Tom Crow, Buddy Marucci, who lost to Tiger Woods in his last amateur, Davis Sezna, an outstanding player, Harcourt Kemp of Louisville, Kentucky, who has played in two U.S. Opens, and Sandy Tatum, former president of USGA, who is now 86 years old. I recently played with him out in California at Cypress Point, which is probably the most beautiful setting of a golf course in the world. I could go on and on, naming people that I have played with at Pine Valley. I'm very happy to say my son Walter was also invited to be a member.

Becoming a member of Pine Valley is analogous to becoming a member of Augusta National, except I think it's even more difficult because becoming a member of the Masters is usually measured by how successful or how much money you have. Members are primarily CEOs of major corporations. But at Pine Valley, which doesn't cost that much to join, they are very selective. The procedure now is that you suggest someone who you think might be a good member, and then he is vetted and investigated thoroughly. Sometimes it takes 10 to 12 years to be invited to join. Lots of times, people never get invited. It took my son 10 years to be invited. They choose whom they want, when they want. It's a very high honor, and one doesn't meet any bad people there. If anyone misbehaves in any way, they write him a letter and sometimes tell him he will not be billed for any further membership.

This has happened to several people over the years. Players had better be on their best behavior at Pine Valley, or risk being invited to go play some place else.

Gordon Brewer is the current president of Pine Valley. Both he and Bill Shean have been senior amateur champions of America twice. I played with them quite a few times, and I love to tell about playing with Bill Shean and David Brookerson, who was then Pennsylvania state champion, Philadelphia city champion and had many other high honors. I was playing with the two of them about 10 years ago, and on the 13th hole—one of the most testing par 4 holes in golf—we had a good wind behind us. I hit a very long drive all the way through the fairway in the direction of the green. Then I hit a 9-iron 150 yards into the hole for an eagle. No one had ever done that before with a 9-iron on the second shot. My feat is written up in the Pine Valley book. That would top a similar experience some 25 years ago where on the same hole I hit a good drive and then hit a 3-wood over 200 yards into the hole for an eagle. I've had two eagles on a par four hole that many people can't even get to in two shots.

Subj: **RE: Super good time as usual with you**
Date: 11/28/2005 6:38:43 PM Eastern Standard Time
From: TATUMFD@cooley.com
To: Franksusieharris@aol.com
Sent from the Internet (Details)

From Sandy (Frank) Tatum Former USGA President and living legion at 86 years old in 2006

Frank,

If there is a better resource for giving life its ultimate dimensions than golf I have not found it. The experiences shared with you at SFGC and Cypress Point are cases in point. If there is a better resource for countering life's doldrums than a sense of humor I have not heard it. I am grateful for being a recipient of yours.

May the birdies proliferate in the New Year.

Sandy

From: Franksusieharris@aol.com [mailto:Franksusieharris@aol.com]
Sent: Sunday, November 27, 2005 10:47 AM
To: Tatum, Sandy
Subject: Super good time as usual with you

Sandy, I mentioned your name yesterday while playing in Naples, Fl. with a friend who also belongs to Inverness and P.V....Jim White.and we had fun telling Tatum stories from planting trees to building golf courses and a reputation unsurpassed.
While I'm personally a little peeved that I can't hit it as far as you at 13-14 years your junior.....I've overcome my failings by masking my grief with efforts at humor, which sometimes creates more grief........WHATEVER......this belated note is to thank you for making the trip to Cypress Point and S.F.Golf another wonderful memory!!
It is pure pleasure to share some time with you any time anywhere.
MERRY CHRISTMAS and A HAPPY-HEALTHY NEW YEAR
Frank (the lesser)

MY EMAIL TO SANDY (FRANK) TATUM. SANDY IS FORMER USGA PRESIDENT AND LIVING LEGEND AT AGE 86 IN 2006.

Subj:
Date: 3/2/2006 8:51:31 PM Eastern Standard Time
From: TATUMFD@cooley.com
To: Franksusieharris@aol.com
Sent from the Internet (Details)

Tempted by an offer of $5000 for my Harding Park First Tee Chapter, I have agreed to give what is denominated as a key note address to a convention of independent insurance agents convening in San Francisco. The subject matter is the efficacy of vision. As I think about it, holding the groups attention for 40 minutes of dissertation and 20 of QandA is a considerable challenge; I will certainly need lightening up and am imposing on your, therefore, to come up with some material. Life continues to be blessedly engaging. If you tune into the Players' Championship telecast you will be startled to see me performing in some Price Waterhouse Coopers commercials in the role of an old coot dispensing core value wisdom to some First Tee kids struggling with the game. In the two days of shooting for four 30 second commercials, notwithstanding the obvious limitations in my thespian talent, I was treated as if I were Clark Gable on location filming Gone With the Wind!

Keep the Faith,

Sandy

Sandy calls on me to help with Humor in his speeches

SANDY'S RESPONSE

Barney Adams, founder of Adams Golf, is a genius in developing clubs. We were partners in a gin rummy game at Pine Valley 30 years ago, and we lost about $40. I said to Barney, "Let's play another game and get the money back."

He said, "Frank, if I lose another $40, I won't be able to get back to Texas." After many lean years trying to make a living in the golf club business, he invented a club called Tight Lies, which was a fantastic design success as a utility club. He took Adams Golf public and made about $20 million. Barney is a great entrepreneur and with a success story in a totally competitive business. He's a good man, and we play golf together frequently. He came to Harbor Springs one summer, rented a cottage and played golf there for several weeks. He's one of the more colorful people, a great friend of Hank Haney, who is the instructor for Tiger Woods, the greatest golfer in the world. Hank and Barney ran a business together.

On one occasion we invited Michael Jordan, probably the greatest basketball player of all time, to Pine Valley. This was prompted by a father-son tournament in which my son, Walter, and I participated along with my friend, Bill Laimbeer, and his son, Billy Laimbeer. Billy was center for the Detroit Pistons at the time. Jordan was then with the Chicago Bulls. Walter had gotten to know Michael Jordan at the

University of North Carolina, where they had enjoyed playing golf together. We wanted to have a match between these two great basketball players.

Michael Jordan invited Ed Ibarguen, his golf coach from the University of North Carolina, to be his father substitute, since his father did not play golf. Michael flew in from California and arrived in a limousine late at night with a girlfriend. Women are not permitted at Pine Valley, so he was refused entrance. However, he came back the next morning after staying at a hotel nearby. As he came in, the maître-d' asked me if it would be all right for him to ask Michael to go meet the kitchen staff, who were primarily black. Michael very graciously did go and shake hands with all the people there, and they were ecstatic.

In one of the matches Michael Jordan was my partner and Billy Laimbeer had a partner who was the head of Occidental Chemical. We had a great match that came down to the 18th hole. I was playing particularly well. Michael played very well until the 18th hole. Then he got into some trees and probably took eight or more shots trying to get to the green. I was on the green in two. Billy Laimbeer, who is seven feet tall, a one-handicap and a better player than I, hit the ball 300 yards back when that was a really big deal. That's done with great regularity on the tour today. I had about a 20-foot putt to win the hole, and I made it. As my putt went in the hole, Michael Jordan sprang at least four or five feet in the air in exhilaration because we won $20 for that putt. He was absolutely delighted.

Michael Jordan was a perfect gentleman when members of the club including board chairmen came over with paper doilies at lunch and asked for his autograph. The chairman of Pine Valley went out and bought two basketballs for Michael to autograph for his grandchildren.

In my first time at the famous Crump Cup at Pine Valley, I drew Dick Siderwroff as an opponent. Ten or 15 years prior to that, he won the British Amateur twice and the American Amateur once. He's about my age, and as we played the very difficult course of Pine Valley. I am very proud to say that I took him to the 16th hole before he closed me out. Bragging rights would have been a lot stronger had I been able to go farther and possibly beat him. I'll never forget what somebody once said to me: People like Siderwroff have an overdrive. When I was winning, he, all of a sudden, began to hit miraculous shots. On the sixth hole (we had played the back nine first), he had a very difficult shot out of the bunker to the right of the green that fell away from him. It was so severely sloped that a ball on the green would almost certainly have rolled off the other side. I'll never forget that shot. He popped it up, put some spin on it, and allowed it to hit just in the edge of the rough, and claw its way down toward the hole to within one foot. If anyone else had hit that shot, it would have been a miracle if it didn't go off the other side of the green.

I could just ramble on forever and ever about golf and where I played and whom I played with. What a life!

ANOTHER WIN AT PINE VALLEY

SPINNING A TALL TALE OR JOKE AT PINE VALLEY

WITH JERRY DIRVEN TO MY RIGHT AND JIM
WHITE TO MY LEFT AT PINE VALLEY

WITH DAN QUAYLE AT PINE VALLEY

26

A New Direction

I n 1985, after promoting myself to CEO/chairman and bringing in Russ Gervais to be the president of AIM Packaging, I had more time on my hands than I could stand. I was only 52 years old and had a lot of cash. I had the opportunity to get into the land development business along Lake Erie with the land around my duck marsh that I had used for customer entertaining and personal enjoyment. After my career in plastic bottle manufacturing, I became a land developer.

I had some experience in developing already with the acquisition of the Spuyten and Duyval Golf Course in Toledo. I bought that with Bob Ebert, along with some small shares for Sam Carter—about 5 percent. This development was a totally leveraged buy for about $400,000 of an existing public golf course. It was strictly a Joe six-pack public course out in the west end of Central Avenue that had been there since the 1920s or earlier. It had good cash flow, which was subject to theft. It was also subject to flooding from a creek that ran through it. No further development was possible. I owned it for about 18 years. After I bought Bob Ebert's share, I had, at the end, 70 percent with the operator, Gary Schanek, having 25 percent and Sam 5 percent. It paid for itself. I never had any cash, just bank loan guarantees, in it and sold it in the late '80s for about $600,000. It provided an interesting possibility for development and whet my interest in that sort of thing.

For the previous 15 years, I had been leasing from Mr. Jack Hankison a 130-acre duck hunting marsh and lodge that we used for customer entertaining and our own entertainment. Some of that property was dry land and was being farmed by the man who took care of our duck marsh, Mr. Al Brunkhorst.

The property consisted of hundreds of lots that were underwater in the marsh and another 50 to 60 that were part of the Sand Beach development, a bit of a run down, though improving, area along Lake Erie in Oak Harbor. I was interested in buying the property for development but the owner, Jack Hankison, did not have a perfectly clear title. The process to clear the title got very complicated. Back in the 1920s Hankinson's father, Otto Hankison, had been in the process of developing and platting all this land. Apparently there was a terrible flood in 1929 just at the start of the Great Depression and the development never fully matured. The marsh was pumped dry at the time of platting, but all the lots filled up after a big storm on Lake Erie. World War II delayed anything further. It was further reduced in value by the development of the Davis Besse Atomic Energy Plant that was built on part of the property and taken by imminent domain.

I got to the point of buying the property subject to clearing the titles of these lots that had been underwater and owned by many different people. Joe Young and Tom Lamarca then approached me to see if I would sell the property. Part of it had a small marina run by Brunkhorst with maybe a 30 or 40-boat marina and the dry farmland. I wanted to know what they wanted to do with it. They told me they were planning to put in channels and develop it into either condominiums or a mobile home park that would allow fishing boats to be parked in front of residences.

At that particular time, Lake Erie had been restored from its near death back in the '50s and '60s when it was so terribly polluted by the industrial waste and sewage that was freely running into it from Detroit and Toledo and the surrounding towns and tributaries that fed it through several rivers. The clean water act had cleared this up and restored excellent fishing. At that time, it was impossible to find a place to dock a boat because dock space in the marinas that had survived the bad days was filled up. There was a hot market for waterfront property where you could park a boat.

Joe Young and Tom Lamarca didn't have the finances to make their dream a reality. However, I became intrigued with the idea of the development that Joe Young had conceived. He is a designer, son of the former head of engineering at Ohio State. He had a great deal of imagination and ability. Tom Lamarca was a real estate sales person who saw the idea of this development as a big opportunity. The more I learned about what they were thinking about doing, the more interested I got. I worked out a deal with them where they would each own 2.5 percent of the project. The project consisted of a huge dryland excavation for channels that were about 10 feet deep and 125 to 150 feet wide. We had to take the spoil and build up the land, which was very low in that area. We would need to get up above the flood plane, thereby providing sites on which you could build condominiums with docks in front. It was a very clever design of land and condos that were small but well built and reasonably priced for sportsmen.

We then began the project by setting up a corporation, which we called Green Cove Development Corporation. I owned about 90 percent. I also laid off—for some guaranteed capital with a couple of other wealthy friends—another 2 or 3 percent as a possibility if I should need any of their capital. I later purchased their small interest.

27

Despite the Blackmail

S o there I was with a new career, and it was a major undertaking. I had no idea how difficult it was to get permits from the myriad permitting authorities that are required—in this case, primarily the Federal Army Corps of Engineers but also, the Ohio Department of Natural Resources, the federal EPA, and the state EPA for both potable water and sewage. It seemed to me that every bureaucratic group had something to say about it, from the possibility of destroying wetlands to habitat for the Indiana bat and the possibility of uncovering of Indian graves.

We began the process of getting the permits from the Corps of Engineers. Joe Young and our engineering firm, whom we eventually hired to do the excavation and put in all of the facilities, assured me that this permit could be acquired. A lot of effort and money was poured into the legal setup of the corporation, the designs, and the submission of plans to the varying authorities. When it looked as if we would not get the permits, I, along with Young and Lamarca, went to Buffalo, New York, to the headquarters of the Corps of Engineers and made a personal appeal with all the logic that we could summon. I sent them a passionate letter as to why this was good for the area, which was under some financial and economic stress. We had the Coast Guard involved there as well. It was an agonizing period of several months. After getting our Congressman, Del Latta, to bring in the Secretary of the Army and Secretary of the Interior, we finally got the permit.

We had to purchase Green Cove Marina from a Mr. Green to provide access and the additional land needed for the development. I made arrangements to buy it for $400,000. This was all subject to obtaining permits. It took almost a year and a lot of legal cost and contacts with all the bureaucracies, but we got the permit and began the excavation of nearly three-quarters of a million cubic yards of spoil.

While we were in the process of moving the dirt, I was in London, England, and I got a telephone call from my lawyer that the Ohio Department of Natural Resources (ODNR) had filed suit for me to cease and desist and to put the land back as it had been. There was a penalty of $25,000 per day if we did not do as they ordered. Though shocked, I had the temerity to say, "To hell with the order. You keep those machines, the drag pans and bulldozers, running. We have the permits." From London, I talked to my attorney, and I talked to the Corps of Engineers. The Corps' position was that the Ohio Department of Natural Resources (ODNR) did not have the authority to stop the project. This was the Corps' prerogative and therefore this was not a valid position for ODNR to take. After talking again from London, at all hours of the day and night, with the Ohio Department of Natural Resources, I was told in so many words, "Well, Mr. Harris, we may not win this lawsuit, but we can certainly run up an awful lot of legal bills for you, and we can keep this thing dormant for 25 years if necessary."

I saw the handwriting on the wall and knew I had to do some compromising. So I called my friend, John B. McCoy, president of Bank One in Columbus at the time, and I asked him if he would contact the head of ODNR and see what compromises could be arranged. This took more time than you can imagine. After I came back from England, and after getting a lot of help from Ohio Director of Economic Development Clarence Pawlicki, I arranged for a meeting with ODNR. Through agonizing negotiations, I was able to get them down from $1 million of remediation to $250,000. This was nothing more than bureaucratic blackmail so that they could go buy some wetlands elsewhere and then get off my back and let the project go forward. I had never stopped the project, and it was going forward with considerable risk that we would not be able to get a sign off from the ODNR.

WITH JOHN B. MCCOY, FORMER CHAIR/CEO BANK
ONE WHEN WE WERE YOUNG PRESIDENTS

It takes guts to win, but you can lose your ass in any risky venture and all business is a risk.

I could write another whole chapter about how we went through the legal meetings and the fight for our rights to develop. It was extremely difficult and expensive, but we pushed forward and essentially had to build a city—a city consisting of over $2 million of electric power necessary to provide the lights and electricity for the condominiums that we intended to build. We had to go through the Ohio EPA for potable drinking water. They were trying to force me to take the water out of ground wells, but the well water was so full of sulfur that it was undrinkable. I spent over $50,000 drilling these unacceptable wells. Then the EPA potable water authority wanted me to build an intake system that would go out hundreds of yards into Lake Erie, which meant I would have to have navigational permits from the

Coast Guard, which would require huge expense—a couple of million or more dollars just to do that. I was finally able to persuade the Ohio EPA to let me use the water that would come into the boat channels, believing that this water would not have the particulate problems of the silt that was kicked up by any storm out in the lake. We were able to do that, subject to their approval of the water quality. I had to contract with the Culligan Company to put in a brand new pressure system for over $750,000 to provide drinking water. It was such a difficult task to get this new equipment approved that I finally had to go to the head of the EPA and essentially get the clerk that I was having to deal with fired before I could get that worked out. We finally got the plant permit for potable drinking water.

The sewage treatment plant and sewer lines, which cost over $1 million, were relatively easy. But its installation required a learning curve that was vertical in my case. Even though we hired consultants, they apparently were unable to sell it very well. I had to learn Waterworks 101 and Sewage Treatment Plants 101 and make the presentation myself to the EPA of Ohio.

Part of the development of Green Cove Condominium Resort was the acquisition of Green's Marina, which had over 300 boat slips and a most unattractive RV park next to where the condominium development was going. We needed to move those RVs to improve the area so the condominium development would not be burdened with the view of it.

I bought another 40 acres of farm land from Green. It was all low land that needed to be raised above the flood plain, because in heavy rains this diked property could end up underwater. I got permits to do that—with the usual agonizing test of fortitude—and put in five ponds of several acres each to raise this land for RV sites with spoil. This created pond view sites for the RVs. Now we have nearly 400 RV sites rented on an annual basis with full services of water, sewer, and electric connections. In addition, another 50 or so mobile homes provide sleeping quarters for the charter fishermen's clients in the marina. We have nearly 75 charter fishermen who bring in people from all over the United States to fish for walleye, bass, and perch.

The nearest store and restaurant was miles away and pretty shabby, so we put in a large Marathon Station with eight pumps for gasoline, a convenience store, a bar and a restaurant, and a marina gas dock on the channel near Lake Erie. That business, which is to support the people who rent the sites for boats and RVs and manufactured homes, is a seasonal business. It has the usual management problems of a place that goes from an absolute boom—jam-packed with people in early spring to late summer—to dropping off terribly when the winter months arrive. Hopefully, all the profits made in the store, restaurant, and bar in the summer is more than enough to keep the key people through the winter.

After digging these channels we then commenced condo construction. In 1986 alone, we built over 200 units of these and sold them as fast as hot cakes for prices that ranged from the least desirable and smallest for around $30,000 to better locations and bigger sizes for around $60,000, which included a boat slip to park up to a 35-foot boat. The business boomed. The demand for fishing, boating sites, and docks was still going at a very high pace. I had borrowed, with personal guarantees, over $5 million from Mid American Bank, now called Sky Bank. The money was beginning to flow very positively. We built these condos as fast as possible with an army of people. The sales were so good that when people came to buy one, we practically had to have them take a number so we could get around to them to show the models. In 1987, we went on to our first sale closing of the first condo building as fast as we could. The building continued with new and bigger designs and higher prices through the late 1980s.

Then more trouble jumped up in the early '90s: the savings and loan debacle. Banks started going broke, and the construction and real estate industry went into the tank big time. Just before that hit, we had done well with the sales and the cash flow, and word of our success had traveled very fast. My good friend, George Haigh, president of Toledo Trust, knew how successful this project was, and wanted our business. So Toledo Trust came out and said they would like to have our business and in order to get it, they would take off my personal guarantees and reduce the interest rate. They got the business! That was an enormous relief to not be in a debtor situation when the "ship hit the sand," so to speak.

The S&L mess stalled the development. I was caught with over 40 units that we had built in anticipation of fast-paced sales and millions of dollars of inventory hanging there in a market that had suddenly gone dead. We struggled through that time, but it took several years before the pace began to pick up again. We have, since the beginning of the project, built and sold nearly 400 condominiums out of a projection of 750 condominiums for the completion.

In 2002 we became a dealer of Fleetwood Manufactured Homes. We have room for about 200 manufactured homes on the land originally planned for condos. These are essentially double-wides of high quality and integrity, since they're built in factories with good quality control. They are uniform in design and color, and the project is now proceeding quite well. We are now selling these units for $90,000 to $120,000 and then renting or leasing a site for them. We're not selling any more land. We are leasing the land and, at an average price per site of $5,000 per year for these manufactured homes, we expect that once we have had the absorption of 200 of them, we will have an income stream of over $1 million a year in today's dollars. At this writing, we have sold about 20. It is a happy situation that will provide, at least for my children and grandchildren, a good income stream.

The usual frustrations of running a cash business, requires an annual audit. Hopefully, people are not stealing too much, although it's certain that some of that goes on. The concern that someone will do something that would endanger your liquor license is always a problem, particularly when a rowdy crowd comes into the bar and gets over-served after having a great time fishing all day. Although we've had very few problems, there is always a concern of what might happen when people drink.

GREEN COVE RESORT AND WILD WINGS MARINA AND R.V. PARK

28

Dodging a Bullet

After I sold AIM Packaging and was spending my winters in Marco Island, Florida, I was concerned that the golf on Marco Island was not all I would like it to be. The golf course on the island, called the Island Country Club, had mostly been a hotel course. Later it became a private country club but was not a particularly good course. The course and the clubhouse have since been improved.

Still, in the Marco Island area there was a need for a nearby private course. There was a public course that was part of the Deltona development of Marco Island and Marco Shores called the Marco Shores Country Club.

I talked to the Deltona people to see if we could buy just the golf course. They were in the process of liquidating their interests in the whole area if they could. They wanted to sell the whole property including the golf course and the development land that was around it. I had negotiations and discussions with Arthur Hills, the famous golf course architect, on what had to be done to the course. He came down and inspected the course. We knew it would require a great deal of water for irrigation, and we knew that was available through the effluent on the island. We also knew we had to bring in an awful lot of new soil to cover up the coral over which they had tried to grow grass. I met with Deltona and negotiated to buy the property for $12 million. I got a contract subject to the approval of the various agencies that required passing on a development—and there were lots of them to convince.

I raised almost 75 percent of the money I needed to renovate the golf course and divide the parcels into single family lots around it. Then, I discovered that there was a new law in Florida, and Collier County in particular, called "concurrency." Concurrency dictated that unless there were adequate roads, electric, and water, you couldn't get a building permit. There was deemed to be a water shortage at that time. After spending $150,000 to $200,000 on legal documents, trying to get permits, spending a year's work raising finances, and after doing all the other preliminary things, we could not get a building permit. The two lane road from Marco Island to U.S. 41—Collier Boulevard—was not adequate for the added traffic. It was terribly congested. Blessedly, I did anticipate that this would not be done fairly soon. It took another 15 years or more before the four-laning of Collier Boulevard took place, allowing for development.

The meter would have been running on that $12 million all that time without any cash flow coming in. I'm glad I missed that one. It could have bankrupted me just trying to hold on. (Although, I would have put it into a separate entity so it couldn't expose me all the way.)

That land is now a renovated Jacobson golf course. They are building high rises on the property that sell for over $1 million each. Once again, timing is everything. The timing was good in that I didn't wade into it and stay too long. The timing was bad in that I didn't have the staying power.

Considering this failure, which was due to circumstances beyond my control, I reflected on other projects I have gotten into. Kenny Rogers' song "The Gambler" holds very true in business: "You got to know when to hold 'em / Know when to fold 'em." You can't keep beating a dead horse, and you certainly can't keep riding one that won't win a race.

29

Various Boards and the IPE

In addition to my own companies, AIM and Green Cove Development Corp., I've been on numerous boards such as the Toledo Humane Society, and the Blue Cross of Ohio Society. Some of the major board positions I have held and organizations that I have served are:

President of the Plastic Bottle Division of the Society of the Plastics Industry.

The board of Brazeway for 19 years, which was one of the best five companies in the world from an industry standpoint. Although it was only about $150 million in sales, it has the best reputation for how it runs its business with Merck and Nestle and others.

The board of Plastic Technologies, a major designer and developer of machinery and equipment for the plastic bottle business.

The board of Minnesota Valley Engineering, largest producer of cryogenic gas vessels.

The board of Continental Glass & Plastics, Chicago, a major packaging distributor.

For over ten years the board of the Institute of Private Enterprise, which is part of the Kenan-Flagler Business School of the University of North Carolina. Some very high-powered businessmen and other luminaries sat on that board including Hugh McColl from Bank of America,

THANK YOU NOTE ON RETIRING AS A BOARD MEMBER OF
BRAZEWAY FROM STEVE HICKMAN, THE CEO/CHAIR

John Medlen CEO of Wachovia, Bill Marriott CEO of Marriott, and others.

The board of the American Senior's Golf Association and the International Senior's Amateur Golf Society.

The board of the Three Score and Ten Gentlemen's Golfers

The board of The Forum Club in Naples, Florida.

The Institute of Private Enterprise, which is part of the Kenan-Flagler Business School of UNC was founded by Professor Rollie Tillman (a classmate of mine) who also had been Vice-Chancellor of UNC. Frank Hawkins Kenan and the Kenan Trust supplied the money to get it started. The concept initially was to promote the Free Enterprise System and recognize that the economic well being of the nation depended on the enterprise of free men and women.

Frank Kenan felt that too many college professors in other disciplines, such as Sociology and Liberal Arts, were unaware of the benefits of free enterprise. In many cases these professors exhibited belligerence towards the economic system that was creating our nation's wealth and well-being. Perhaps a solution would be to provide an opportunity for college professors to meet and get to know successful business people. And thus the Institute of Private Enterprise was born.

Rollie Tillman, through enormous effort and persuasion, brought together over 24 top business leaders from around the nation to form the original board of IPE. I was honored to be asked to be a founding member and to represent entrepreneurial small business. We accomplished much to help free enterprise thrive, including the establishment of a large corps of MBAs who went to eastern Europe to teach the basics of business to the emerging countries from communism.

A separate book could be written on the IPE and the successes it has had.

General Administration Building. The papers will be transferred to the University Library in 1987.

Entrepreneur returns as executive-in-residence

Frank Harris '55 told business students at his alma mater his saga of starting a high risk business, making it a success, selling out, and then buying it back — twice. The company Harris built and now heads as CEO and chairman of the board is Aim Packaging, Inc., a Port Clinton, Ohio manufacturer of plastic bottles for giants like Procter & Gamble, Helene Curtis, Bristol-Myers and other makers of toiletries, drugs, foods and beverages.

Harris was a January executive-in-residence at the School of Business Administration's new Institute of Private Enterprise which was funded by the William R. Kenan Charitable Trust. Harris serves on the Institute's 22-member board of trustees, which includes some of the country's most prominent corporate executives.

Although he had a successful 14-year sales management career with a major container manufacturer, Harris wasn't getting what he wanted. "I had paid my dues and didn't get the brass ring," he told students, and that led to founding his own plastics company, which was eventually acquired by a conglomerate.

Buying it back five years later with new partners created another problem when they sold out their controlling interest within two years to another party, but Harris was able to regain ownership.

Harris, a native of Lincolnton, N.C., has passed along his fascination for business to his son Walter, who is currently at UNC working on his M.B.A. degree.

First $1 million chair endowed

The Morehead Alumni Distinguished Professorship, the first endowed at $1 million, has been

WRITE-UP IN THE *CAROLINA ALUMNI REVIEW*, WINTER 1987

Frank Harris, January executive-in-residence at the Institute of Private Enterprise, tells business students about his experience as an entrepreneur.

The Kenan-Flagler Business School
The University of North Carolina
  at Chapel Hill
Campus Box 3490, McColl Building
Chapel Hill, NC 27599-3490 USA

March 30, 1999

Mr. Frank M. Harris
710 Buttonbush Lane
Naples, FL 34108

Dear Frank:

I am slow in replying to your phone messages and letter of March 19, but not for lack of appreciation for what your years of advice and support have meant to me personally and to the Kenan Institute as we grew it from a vague idea to a working force for UNC. I can't begin to thank you for all your steadfast encouragement. Besides, it's just plain fun to be with you two.

But I understand that conflicts crop up, and have dropped off a couple of boards this year because I couldn't seem to get there, and didn't feel right about it.

Still, I hope that you will remember that your service as a charter Trustee and your membership in the UNC Alumni family guarantees that the welcome mat stays perpetually out for you and Susie in Chapel Hill. The Tillmans, the Evans (and, as always your loving fans in the development office!) want to know that we will see you on this Hill whenever you can make it this way.

Best to you both.

Sincerely,

Rollie Tillman
H. Allen Andrew Professor of Entrepreneurship

WITH CONSIDERABLE REGRETS I RESIGNED FROM
THE IPE IN 1999 DUE TO TIME CONSTRAINTS

30

YPO and a Special Friend, Gary Player

I became a member of the Young President's Organization (YPO) in 1970 or 1971 and was a social chairman in the Maumee Valley Chapter of this worldwide organization of presidents who ran businesses of adequate size—in our case, the manufacturing business. When I got in, there was a $5 million annual sales minimum, and you had to be a Young President before you were 40 to be admitted. I was quite active and went to many of their universities held in, for instance, Mexico, the United States, Canada, Japan, and Australia. I met many intelligent people who were available for help as needed. Upon matriculating to age 50 in YPO, you are thrown out as a Young President but invited to join YPO-49. About 10 percent of the active YPO people over 50 who have demonstrated leadership qualities within YPO are invited to join the Chief Executives Organization (CEO). I am highly honored and proud to have been invited into the CEO. I have attended many of the forums in various parts of the world, including Japan, South Africa, Australia, Spain, and Canada.

A wonderful experience occurred in one of our CEO forums in South Africa about 10 years ago, back in the mid-1990s. As we were preparing to take the trip, I decided to play some of the better golf courses there. I had the temerity to call the number listed in the Pine Valley Roster for Gary Player, one of the most famous golfers of all time, a world-renowned player from South Africa and a member of Pine Valley. Gary's won everything there is to be won from the Masters, the Open, and the PGAs. I had seen his name on the roster, but I had never met him. The phone number turned out to be Sports Management in Cleveland, and I got his coordinator, a woman. I told her I was a member of Pine Valley, I was going to South Africa and wondered if she could help me arrange to play golf at some of the better clubs in Johannesburg and Cape Town while I was there. She responded that she would have Mr. Player call me. I thought to myself, "Well, that's the end of that."

About 20 minutes later, Gary Player called me. We had a wonderful chat about Pine Valley, members there that he knew, and especially the president of the club, Mel Dickenson, of whom he thought highly. He called me "Mr. Harris." He did not call me "Frank." He finally said, "Mr. Harris," in a very gracious tone, "what can I do for you? I'd love to help you."

I told him I would like to play some of the better courses in South Africa, and he said, "Well, now, if you'll fax me when you're going to be where and when you would like to play and how many of you would like to play, I'll make those arrangements for you. And I'll fax back to you the names of the people in my organization in South Africa that will do whatever is necessary to make you comfortable and enjoy your trip."

I said, "Gosh, Gary, I don't have any friends that good. You're just wonderful to offer to do this." Well, as it turns out, he called back at least two other times. I had at least three other faxes from his people in South Africa. The arrangements were made. We couldn't even pay greens fees. We were received like royalty under his auspices at four different wonderful clubs in Johannesburg and Cape Town. I wrote him before I left to say how much I appreciated all he'd done to set up the trip. The people in South Africa were enormously gracious to all of us CEO members. I wrote at least 10 letters thanking people for their kindness—people I played with and dined with in their homes, very elegant people.

While we were there, we had Nelson Mandela and F. W. de Klerk speak to us. It was just great. We met so many wonderful people there and for some dumb reason, I forgot to write Gary Player when I got back. A month or two later, I read in a magazine that he had just turned 60.

I said, "Oh, my God, I need to write Gary Player."

I wrote a two-page letter explaining what a wonderful time I'd had and how once you get to 60 some of your memory, like your putting stroke, disappears. I couldn't thank him enough for his kindness. The remarkable thing about that was he picked up the phone and called me to thank me for thanking him. I thought, "What a guy!" When he was playing in one of the tournaments in Naples, I slipped my card to his caddie as I was standing in the gallery.

His caddy gave it to him, and he came over and said, "I'm so glad to meet you in person, Mr. Harris."

What a guy!

31

Hunting and Fishing

After we got married, I found that Susie's father loved to hunt and shoot pheasants. Pheasant hunting was something that didn't happen in North Carolina. On special trips we would go to Mr. Draper's hunting club to shoot pheasants and watch

WITH GOOD FRIENDS FISHING IN ALASKA. IN FRONT
OF ME ARE PAT AND BOB EBERT AND THEN SUSIE.

handsome bird dogs work the fields. On one occasion we hunted with the chairman of the board of Owens Corning, Harold Boeschenstein. He had the fanciest shotgun I'd ever seen. I shot with other prominent people around Toledo, like John Hill, who eventually became the president of Aetna Life Insurance Company in Hartford. I got to know some good friends, people who had access to private hunting clubs and who took hunting trips. I fell in with that group of fun-to-be-with people who also usually played golf, tennis, shot birds, and took wonderful fishing and hunting trips. I really developed a passion for that sort of recreation and the camaraderie of those bright people.

GOOSE HUNTING TRIP TO BELCHER ISLAND, 1973.
(A) TONY BARNUM'S MALLARD AIRPLANE WHICH WE
NEARLY CRASHED MY LAST TRIP WITH HIM. (B) TO MY
LEFT ARE TOM SWIGART, JOHN KERN AND BOB EBERT.

Susie and I have fished all over the world. One of our favorite spots was the Fishing Unlimited Camp on Lake Clark in Alaska about an hour's flight out of Anchorage. There are dozens of streams that we'd fly to from the camp, such as to Kodiak Island and Suliac Island, where we fished for salmon, char, and rainbow trout. Others come to mind in Chile and Argentina. We've deep-sea fished off the coast of Mexico and fished in Canada for Atlantic salmon on the Whale River in Newfoundland and then Quebec, in pontoon planes while I was there with the former chairman of Toledo Scale, Harris Macintosh, and a bunch of other wonderful people from Toledo who invited my son, Walter, along with me.

FISHING IN ALASKA

I'll never forget our first time fishing for salmon in Alaska. We were fishing along the stream, and a huge, almost blonde Kodiak bear suddenly came within 200 yards of us. He stood up, and he must have been eight feet tall. Our guide said we better move away from the stream and just leave the salmon we caught there. Don't ever hook a salmon onto your body or carry one, because bears have very poor eyesight but a keen sense of smell. They are at the top of their food chain, and you don't ever want a bear confusing you with part of his chain. They can outrun you.

The guide told us to move away cautiously, all the while talking to the bear, and letting the bear get whatever he wanted. We had hardly been told that when the bear approached. We were talking to him. The guide told us to put a little more space between us. He told us to walk fast—not run—away from the bear. We were in waders, and we trudged into a marshy area. My short-wheeled wife was about 30 or 40 yards behind me, and I said, "You know, honey, I don't have to outrun that bear. I just have to outrun you. I think you'd better pick it up a little bit." Her little legs were churning as hard as they could go through the marsh grass.

Dick and Sissy King were in our party. Dick King is of the King Ranch Family. They were wonderful friends. Sissy hunted and fished along with Jan Myers, wife of Miller Myers, the CEO of the Dairy

MILLER MEYERS, FORMER HEAD OF DAIRY QUEEN
INTERNATIONAL, IN ALASKA, 1993

Queen Company. We always had to help the ladies up onto the plane's pontoons and off again so they could get in and out of the plane. They always stayed close to the plane, wading maybe 50 or so yards away. We men went farther and farther up the streams to find a place that had not been over fished. We had to get up very early in the morning to fly in to the good fishing spots. If we didn't get there early, there was another airplane that had flown in from another camp.

So Jan Myers and Sissy King were fishing near the airplane and Sissy King said to Jan, "You know, I think we should be talking."

Jan said, "What do you mean?"

ALASKA 1994

"There's a bear right over there." The bear was probably 30 yards away. They started to talk and move toward the airplane. Amazingly, these two ladies jumped up on that pontoon and hopped into the airplane without any assistance at all. That was a great story to tell back at camp. They sat in that airplane until we all came back from fishing, hours later.

Where we lived on Marco Island on the Marco River, our next door neighbor was retired General William Patch. He had come from an extremely distinguished Army family. His great grandfather was married to Minerva King, and that's how we got involved with the King Ranch Family. General Patch's grandfather was a war hero in World War I, and his father was a very famous general under Patton in World War II.

OUR HOUSE AT 227 POLYNESIA COURT, MARCO
ISLAND WHICH WE HAD BUILT AND WHERE
WE LIVED PART TIME FOR 20 YEARS

CHRISTMAS ON MARCO ISLAND IN THE '70S

ANOTHER
GOOD DAY
IN THE GULF
OF MEXICO
OUT FROM
NAPLES/
MARCO

ANOTHER
GOOD CATCH

TOOK SON WALTER
FOR A BIG DAY OF
TARPON FISHING

ON ONE OF MANY VISITS TO THE KING RANCH

General Patch loved to fish throughout the Ten Thousand Islands south of Marco Island. He knew Sir Gregor McGregor, the head of the clan in Scotland, because Patch had served with him in Europe. Sir McGregor was an imposing, huge man with blond mane and moustache, the essence of British-Scottish nobility. Sir McGregor invited General Patch to 'cross the pond' and participate in grouse shooting in Scotland. He invited me to come along. We flew to Edinburgh, Scotland, and then drove down to a town called Kelso on the Tweed River. From there we shot grouse for a week in the Lamimuirs, the moors between Kelso and Edinburgh.

This was gentlemanly hunting that I had never experienced. People wore beautiful, colorful tweed coats and ties, some that had belonged to their grandfathers and they said last forever. They could stand in the rain with this very tightly woven, almost waterproof wool.

The shoot had a huge cast of about 30 beaters. The beaters go out two miles strung out 25 yards apart. With snapping white flags on a

GROUSE SHOOTING IN SCOTLAND

stick, they drove the grouse toward us. We were stationed in a blind, which is called a butt and sunk in the ground and often made of stone. Some have been there for a century or more. As the birds were driven toward us, they were flying at high speed. Grouse are about the size of a city pigeon and were the most difficult shooting. When that bird was 100 yards out we had to pick the spot where we thought it was going to be and shoot, because by the time we got our guns up to shoot, the bird was within 40 yards of us, closing fast. If we waited too long, he passed us. Then, we whirled around and tried to shoot him going away, and that was equally difficult. I threw my back out trying to do that. I was a good shot, but I never imagined shooting that tough. I got a write-up in one of the sporting magazines. They quoted me as saying I thought I was a pretty good shot until I experienced the shooting of grouse.

Given the grand scene, I had two shotguns and a loader. These were double-barrel guns only—side by sides or over and unders. I have some very good American guns—beautiful, highly engraved Winchester 21s—but the Scots turned up their noses at them because it wasn't of the craftsmanship they favored. The Brits made wonderful shotguns, and many of them were very expensive, costing more than a good car.

There would be a line of eight of these butts, and numbers were drawn to determine your particular butt. Sometimes the birds would go to one end more prevalently than the other, and the shooting was great only on one end. I was able to move up a number with each drive, and there would be about eight drives per day, each drive lasting only 10 to 15 minutes. We would move to other lines of these butts within a mile or so after each drive. After the morning drives of three or four, we had a luncheon in the field on a table cloth off the back of Land Rovers. It was spectacular—smoked salmon, every kind of wonderful meat I could imagine, vegetables, fruit, every kind of cake and cookie, and wine. I was brought up never, ever to drink when shooting, but we really had a full measure of wine and port in Scotland.

When we shot grouse, a group of people called pickers collected the birds from the heather. They had magnificent Labradors and other kinds of dogs that found the grouse for the pickers. It was very ceremonial. The beaters and pickers were fed at different places than we shooters. We stood around eating, drinking and telling jokes while we ate lunch. Usually we'd find a place to take a quick little nap, because it'd been a long time since we left the hotel.

Dick King was General Patch's first cousin, and Dick and Sissy were there. George and Hattie Urschel were friends from Toledo who went with us. Every night we donned coat and tie for fancy cocktails and dinner. It was an uproariously good time, with people telling stories and jokes. I probably know 2,000 jokes, so I had the opportunity to perform there as at other places. After a while, if you tell jokes, people will feed you jokes. It's a vicious cycle that goes on and on.

We became good friends with the King family, who invited us and the Urschels to come to their ranch and shoot quail. Truly, nothing is fancier than the shooting in Scotland, but Dick and Sissy's ranch is huge—28 miles in one direction and 18 in another. Hebbronville, in Texas down near the Mexican border, is known as one of the best places for bobwhite quail in the world.

They had the most beautiful bird dogs I've ever seen. We'd go out in Suburbans. The dogs would be put out of the trailer, and they would run over 20 or 30 acres of mesquite and cactus fields. When they smelled quail, they would slam on a point. We would approach and then have a covey of eight to 18 quail flush into the sky. Quail shooting is extremely fast. You'd better be a good shot, or you'll never hit a quail when they flush. We would hunt up the singles and then wait for the dogs to find another covey. In North Carolina, if you hunt quail, you might see three coveys in a day of long walks and with good dogs to find them. At the King ranch, we found about 30 coveys in one day.

We hunted quail for 20 years with the Kings. Every year we were invited back, and we were allowed to bring other couples to hunt and be entertained by the Kings and to golf in Corpus Christie. Over the years we went there with the following friends: George & Hattie Urschel, Jim & Sue White, PJ & Jean Johnson, Rusty & Nancy Heyman, Tom & Peggy Walbridge, Greg & "H" Emmert, Bill & Linda Macartney, Miller & Jan Meyers, Bernie & Ellie Baker, Dan & Nancy Ferguson, Hardwick & Betsy Cauldwell. The Kings entertained us as soon as we got off the plane with a wonderful luncheon at the Corpus Christi Yacht Club. Then we would go to the ranch and have wonderful dinners every night. They had the best cooks and service.

One of the greatest hunting trips Susie and I had was with General Patch's son, Billy. I had entertained him at my hunting marsh, and he shot grouse with us in Scotland. Billy came up with the idea for a trip to Spain to shoot red leg partridge. It was the same as in Scotland—driving birds across rather arid country in the central part of Spain. Also on the trip were Dick and Sissy King and couples from Toledo, Ohio— Philip and Phe Laboutillier, Bernie and Ellie Baker, Bill and Kay Stokley, and Henry and Billy Grace Goodrich. I was able to take my daughter, Gingi, and son, Walter. Gingi, along with some of the other women, did not shoot, but they entertained themselves at the museums in Madrid, shopping and sightseeing. There were probably twice as many driven partridges in Spain as there were in Scotland's grouse shoots, so the shooting was fast and furious. It was $1,000 a day per person to shoot, and the facilities where we stayed were wonderful.

All my life, anything to do with sports, hunting and fishing was a great pleasure to me.

OUR GOOD
FRIENDS DICK
AND SISSY KING

SUSIE WITH
SHOTGUN AT
KING'S RANCH

KING AND QUEEN AT BUNRATTY CASTLE
IRELAND DURING OUR FIRST VISIT AS
GUESTS OF THE IRISH GOVERNMENT

32

Golf: Good Friends, Wonderful Places

It's said that you can tell a man's character by how he acts and handles himself on a golf course.

The beauty of golf is that the rules are very clear, though complicated, and every man polices himself. If you cheat at golf, there's no gain. Golfers call rules on themselves—something that was drilled into me very early. Throughout my life, I exposed myself to golf as much as I could afford it. I have golfed in most of the United States, in the British Isles, Spain, Portugal, Holland, Germany, Denmark, Italy,

GOLF SWING AND FOLLOW THROUGH

Bermuda, Mexico, Argentina, Brazil, the Caribbean Islands, Canada, Hawaii, New Zealand, Australia, Singapore, Japan, China, Hong Kong, Thailand, France, Belgium, and South Africa. Golf has taken my wife and me on a wonderful ride throughout the world, and it continues to be our passion.

One of the great thrills in golf is to get a hole-in-one. To date I've had that experience eight times. The first was with Greg and Helen Emmert at Ocean Reef around 1980. The longest hole-in-one was at Camargo Club Cimci in 2006 as Jerry Dirvin's guest—180 yards with a four iron. I've had many eagles on par fives as well as quite a few on par fours. The best eagles were two at Pine Valley's Number 13, twenty years apart. The first was with a three wood on the second shot. The second time was with a nine iron.

Since 1977, I've won club championships in every club I've ever belonged to, about 20 altogether. Within the last 10 years, I have been club champion at the Wilderness Club, the Hole in the Wall Club, and Royal Poinciana—all of which are in Naples. I was champion the same year at all three clubs. Those clubs are all contiguous to each other on Goodlette-Frank Road in Naples. I used to say I've got 72 holes of golf I can get to without going out on the street. I've won four times at Hole in the Wall Club. At Royal Poinciana I was the 2005 club champion at age 72 after winning seven times.

Winning club championships is certainly not the highest honor in playing amateur golf. Winning state championships, city championships, and national championships for amateurs are the bigger stepping stones for recognition. Any competition is fun.

The ascendance to playing in a club championship final is done two ways. In match play, there's an elimination process where the first 16 lowest qualifiers get to play. We then play off the better qualifiers, playing against the worst qualifiers until we get down to the semi-finals and the finals if we survive that. Occasionally, the worst qualifiers will rise all the way to the top. So match play is a many splendored thing. Some days you're good, some days you're off.

The other method is medal play. Medal play is not going against man to man, but it's going against the field of golfers like most professional golf events. Sometimes it's 54 holes. The club championship at Royal Poinciana is 36 holes in two days. So you go out, and you shoot the best you can, and then you see how the rest of the group on the field did. There can be a playoff if you're tied at the end of 36 holes. The first three or four championships at RP were match play, and the last three or four have been medal play.

In 2001, after having an absolutely terrific first 18 holes, I shot even par and was ahead of the field by four or five shots. The next day, the first nine holes I shot six over par, and my body was just not performing at all. I thought, "My God, I've blown this whole tournament." So I went into the locker room after nine holes and drank two beers. I said, "There's something wrong here." That settled me down, and I was able to go out and shoot even par on the last nine holes. I'm not recommending that you drink and play, but in this particular instance it seemed to help. I won by one shot, beating a fellow named John Teller with whom I had been tied.

That story is like the story of my first club championship at Belmont Country Club in Toledo (see Chapter 21). I hit my drive on the 18th hole into the fairway sand trap. John had a par. Then I hit an 8-iron onto the green and sunk a 20-foot putt for a birdie. There were 50 people watching, and it was quite exhilarating. I've had quite a few come-from-behind experiences. It's like magic. Protecting a lead in golf is very difficult. Many times, the players on the professional tour going into the last round of the day will have a three or four stroke lead, and they'll go out and shoot terribly, trying to protect it. Then, some guy with no chance of winning is just out there swinging free with all to gain and nothing to lose. He makes spectacular shots and comes from behind to win.

There are myriad golf courses and clubs that are outstanding in aesthetics, beauty, and golfability. They're all over the world, and I've played many of them. The ones that stimulate your "God!-I'm-glad-to-be-here" attitude are those where major competitive events have been held, such as U.S. Opens and PGAs—events that you've watched on television. You get that feeling at clubs like Marion in Ardmore, Pennsylvania, where quite a few Opens have been held. Ben Hogan won there. Others are Inverness in Toledo, Ohio, which has had four Opens and two PGAs and innumerable other invitationals, where the Sam Sneads and the Byron Nelsons and the other great players of the '20s, '30s and '40s played. Byron Nelson was the pro at the Inverness Club in Toledo when he won 11 straight PGA tournaments—a record nobody will ever achieve again, although as I write this Tiger Woods has just achieved seven in a row. There's Baltusrol in Summit, New Jersey, Oakmont outside of Pittsburg, Oakland Hills outside of Detroit, Pebble Beach in California—all wonderful golf courses that have stood the test of time as great tests of a golfer's skill. When you go to the places where the great events have been held, that certainly makes it singularly special.

And golf is not just the places. They are magnificent in their aesthetics and location, but it's not just those places where wonderful events have been held, and it's not just the physical aspect of golf. It's truly the spiritual aspect of golf as it relates to the love of the game and the people with whom you play the game. There's a camaraderie that isn't matched in any other sport. I have played almost all sports at some level, including team sports, but the individual sports of fishing, hunting, and golf are where the camaraderie is best—sharing those experiences in a beautiful stream or lake, catching beautiful fish, field shooting with bird dogs that are magnificent to watch. It's the Labrador retriever that absolutely fills your heart with joy. When you're able to shoot a duck, the duck falls in the weeds, and you send a well-trained dog out to get the duck. He doesn't get the scent because the wind's blowing the wrong direction. He's going in the wrong direction. You blow the whistle and he turns around and looks at you. You give him a hand signal to the right, and he will go to the right. He goes too far, so you blow the whistle again. He'll look at you again, and you wave him back the other way. Then if he's not deep enough, you blow the whistle again. He'll look at you, and you wave your hand up over your head and the dog goes deeper in. He picks up the duck once he gets to the scent. He swims back to the blind, and he's so proud of himself. It's the super bowl for a Labrador retriever. It's a marvelous experience that fills your heart.

BECKY, 1980, MY FIRST LABRADOR RETRIEVER

NESSIE, A GOOD BLACK LAB   HAWK, THE LAST AND BEST

But when you're playing golf with friends—and this happens for me several times a week—somebody makes a fabulous shot, and everybody's happy. A lot of times I play with guys who are in their 20s and 30s and beat them. I occasionally out-drive some much younger men. One of my great lines that I use frequently when I'm playing with younger guys, usually those who are in their 50s and I out-drive them, I say to them, "Don't worry. When you get a little older, you'll be able to hit it farther." You've done something that they haven't been able to do, whether it's blasting the ball out of a sand trap or hitting a good shot. In golf, amazingly, you applaud your opponents' good shots. You don't ever say, "That's a terrible shot," to somebody, unless you're just good friends and you're needling them. When somebody hits a good shot even on the Pro Tour, their opponents will say "good shot" or "nice putt." It's a warm and fuzzy thing to be with people you enjoy. You talk about the world and your jobs and such things. Playing with people who love the game—sophisticated business people, professors, college presidents—can be very interesting.

THANK YOU NOTE FROM GENE SARAZEN WITH
WHOM I ONCE PLAYED 18 HOLES

One "Great Day" Dr. Gordon Brewer Former US Senior Amateur Champ on his Course

RATINGS Course / Slope										
Mens Blue: 74.6 / 137 Dark Green: 71.7 / 130 Light Green: 69.5 / 124 **Ladies** Yellow: 72.1 / 125 Red: 68.8 / 118										

LEGEND Emergency Phone · Restroom & Shelter

HOLE	1	2	3	4	5	6	7	8	9	OUT
BLUE TEES	396	434	189	547	367	461	563	224	421	3602
DARK GREEN TEES	350	405	167	517	334	434	535	195	394	3331
LIGHT GREEN TEES	322	375	147	486	307	406	511	172	365	3091
MENS HANDICAP	11	7	17	5	13	1	3	15	9	
Frank	4	4	(2)	4	4	4	5	4	5	36
Jordan (Brewer)	4	4	4	4	5	4	5	3	3	36
PAR	4	4	3	5	4	4	5	3	4	36
LADIES HANDICAP	11	5	17	1	13	9	3	15	7	
RED TEES	264	316	94	427	250	350	418	125	313	2557

RATINGS Course / Slope												
Mens Blue: 74.6 / 137 Dark Green: 71.7 / 130 Light Green: 69.5 / 124 **Ladies** Yellow: 72.1 / 125 Red: 68.8 / 118												

LEGEND Emergency Phone · Restroom & Shelter

HOLE	10	11	12	13	14	15	16	17	18	IN	TOT	HCP	NET
BLUE TEES	201	580	437	195	423	517	352	204	527	3436	7038		
DARK GREEN TEES	185	553	382	166	392	490	327	181	502	3178	6509		
LIGHT GREEN TEES	166	523	360	137	369	461	300	150	472	2938	6029		
MENS HANDICAP	14	2	4	18	10	8	12	16	6				
Frank	4	5	3	3	4	5	5	3	5	37	73		
Jordan (Brewer)	3	7	4	3	4	5	4	3	5	38	74		
PAR	3	5	4	3	4	5	4	3	5	36	72		
LADIES HANDICAP	14	2	10	18	8	6	12	16	4				
RED TEES	113	425	306	89	314	413	244	95	414	2413	4970		

ONE "GREAT DAY." BEAT GORDON BREWER, FORMER
U.S. SENIOR AMATEUR CHAMP ON HIS COURSE.

One of my more colorful friends was General Jim Murray, probably one of the most personable people I ever met. He was from Newton, North Carolina, 15 miles from my hometown of Lincolnton. He had become president of Teledyne Aviation Engines and was a producer of cruise missile engines in Toledo. He invited me to go to the Lake of the Ozarks on his private King Air airplane to a meeting of the Conquistador del Cielo, or Conquerors of the Skies. At that meeting was every president of just about every major airline in the world. Also there was the chairman of Rolls Royce and General Electric, and Dick Farris of United Airlines. On the flight out there, we picked up the head of North American Rockwell in Dayton. At that same stop, we picked up Neil Armstrong, the first man on the moon.

We flew out to the Lake of the Ozarks, and I was surrounded by luminaries from all over the United States—astronauts, test pilots, and people who ran aerospace companies. I got to know Neil Armstrong as well as one can get to know a very shy and retiring sort of man. I got to play golf with him. He was not a very good golfer, and he is far from a conversationalist. He was very modest and pleasant. I remember, with my usual smart mouth, saying to him, after he hit a ball across a ditch and jumped over the ditch, "That was one great leap for mankind." He looked at me like, "Why would you mention something like that?" We had a good time, and I was very pleased to get to know him. We discussed his coming up and shooting ducks with me. I called him several times for it. He was a professor of aeronautical engineering at the University of Cincinnati at that time after retiring from NASA. Unfortunately, we never got together again.

I was on the Board of the Institute of Private Enterprise, University of North Carolina, which was chaired by the dean of the business school, the former vice chairman of IBM, Paul Rizzo. Rizzo invited me, Paul Harden, chancellor of the university, and Billy Armfield to Augusta National to play for a couple of days. I shot a 75 the first time I ever played the golf course. I was thrilled to play so well on such a difficult golf course. As we were having dinner that night, they were talking about who was going to give substantial amounts of money to the University of North Carolina to celebrate its bicentennial.

Julian Robertson, a classmate of mine who made billions of dollars in the Tiger Fund, was going to give $5 million to $10 million. John Belk of the department stores was going to give $2 million. Others were going to give hundreds of thousands. Paul Rizzo turned to me at the dinner table and said, "Frank, what are you going to do with all your money?"

I suspected this was coming, so I was prepared. I said, "Paul, this reminds me of my former next door neighbor down on Marco Island, General Patch, who told the story of when he was a major in the Korean War. He and a company of soldiers were pinned down in a ditch with a Chinese machine gun up on a hill. They had been there for about half a day, and Major Patch turned to this black sergeant and said, 'Sergeant, get up there and take that machine gun.' The sergeant looked at him and said, "Yes, sir, major, that's a good idea, but they ain't finished using it.'"

Rizzo said, "I got your message. You ain't finished using your money yet."

I was able to return to Augusta National another time with Bill Boeschenstein, the former chairman of Owens Corning, and his wife, Molly. Susie and I had a wonderful time playing golf while staying in the Eisenhower Cottage. These things are so much fun because you hear about them on TV and in writings about the great contests which have gone on at the Masters. It's a unique golf experience, almost a Sistine Chapel of golf by the reverence, the way the players act, and certainly the way the fans act. You don't have unruly fans. The place is absolutely magnificent.

My third visit to Augusta National was in February 2007 with Jim White, his son Jimmy and club member Clay Boardman. We had beautiful weather, some good golf shots (I almost had a hole-in-one at Number 16) and a lot of bad ones.

Hord Harden was the czar of Augusta National for many years, and after his retirement we were on the greens committee together at the Hole in the Wall Golf Club in Naples. When I came back from playing Augusta with Bill Boeschenstein, I said, "Hord, I can't believe how you make that grass so green. The place is just luminescent. The grass is so magnificent."

Hord, who was always irreverent, said, "Hell, it ought to be green. We got 90 acres of grass out there and we put on 90 thousand pounds of seed and fertilizer every year. We have an unlimited budget, and we usually exceed it."

Hord was a very strong-willed guy who ran Augusta National with an iron hand after Clifford Roberts, the tyrant of Augusta, died. Robert Tyree Jones was one of the architects, along with McKinsey. They built that course back in the 1920s.

Golf Digest

Ron Whitten
Architecture Editor

May 11, 1999

Mr. Frank M. Harris
1714 River Rd.,
Maumee, Ohio 43537

Dear Frank,

It is with regret that we accept your resignation as a GOLF DIGEST panelist, but we understand the circumstances.

Please accept our gratitude for the many years you've spent evaluating courses for GOLF DIGEST. Our golf course rankings benefited from your participation.

Best wishes,

Ron Whitten
Architecture Editor
GOLF DIGEST

REW/lgw

ACCEPTANCE OF MY RESIGNATION FROM
BEING A *GOLF DIGEST* PANELIST

I was elected to the *Golf Digest Magazine* panel to help choose the top 100 golf courses in the United States. I was on that panel for 10 or 12 years traveling and being comped at many wonderful places to rank those golf courses—old and new. It got to be hard work. I had to rank 12 of them a year and some of them were not that good. Extensive travel was required at my own expense, although I usually got free greens fees for one or two of us to play.

While I was at our cottage in Northern Michigan, I was invited to play with Steve Kircher, owner of Boyne and Jim Frank, the editor of *Golf Magazine*. I told him I had been on the *Golf Digest* panel and that I was getting a little tired of having to do that many reviews. He invited me to be on the *Golf Magazine* panel and rank as many as I wanted to which I did for about four years.

As a member of that panel in 2002 I was invited to go to Jeju Island in Korea, the Nine Bridges Golf Course, to be part of, but not to play, in the First World Club Championship, which consisted of players from all over the United States, England, Scotland, Ireland, and Australia. It was an all expense paid, first class trip as the guest of Mr. Lee, son the founder of Samsung. As I write this in 2007 I have just received an invitation to go again to Korea/Jeju as their guest and be a panelist again for *Golf Magazine*. Wow!

Any discussion about the passion of golf would be incomplete without mentioning the beginnings of golf in Scotland at St. Andrews, the Royal & Ancient Club there, and Muirfield.

St Andrews Links in the city of St Andrews, Scotland, is regarded as the "home of golf." Golf has been played there ever since the 15th century. Today there are six public golf courses including the Old Course, which are widely considered to be among the finest, and certainly the most famous and traditional, courses in the world. The courses of St Andrews Links are owned by the local authorities and operated by St Andrews Links Trust, a charitable organization. St Andrews is also home to the Royal and Ancient Golf Club of St Andrews, one of the most prestigious golf clubs and one of the ruling authorities of golf.

The Honourable Company of Edinburgh Golfers is the longest established golf club in the world, although the game of golf is several centuries older. The club's records date back to 1744 when it produced 13 "Rules of Golf" for its first competition, which was played for the Silver Club. The club played on the five holes at Leith Links for nearly a century, but in 1836 it moved to Musselburgh's 9-hole Old Course. Like many prestigious Scottish courses, including St. Andrews, Musselburgh is a public course, and in 1891 the club built a private course at Muirfield.

Muirfield has hosted The Open Championship 15 times, most recently in 2002, The Amateur Championship, the Ryder Cup, the Walker Cup, the Curtis Cup and many other tournaments.

I had been introduced by letter to the captains of St. Andrews and Muirfield. The Muirfield captain was Paddy Hamner, who has the reputation as being one of the meanest people in the world. My letter of introduction was from the president of Pine Valley. Paddy replied in the letter that I should call when I was in the area to reconfirm. So, after a day off from shooting grouse, Hattie and George Urschel and my wife and I planned to go to Muirfield. I called from the town where we were staying on the Tweed River. I said to Captain Hamner, "I would like to reconfirm my tee time."

He screamed into the phone, "We have no tee times at Muirfield!"

Knowing his reputation, I said "Captain Hamner, I got your nice letter suggesting I call, and whatever time is convenient for you would be fine for us." Thinking fast I continued, "By the way, we've been shooting grouse down here in the Lamamuirs, and we have more grouse than we can possibly use. Would you like to have some?"

"Oh," he said, "that would be very nice."

So I packed a beer case with about two dozen grouse, and arrived at Captain Hamner's office with my tweed cap on, trying to look as Scottish as possible. His assistant ushered me into the office, which was a cluttered mess. He had an old Labrador retriever in there that looked like he hadn't had a bath in 10 years. The assistant said "Take your hat off, take your hat off."

I said, "You take it off. My hands are full of grouse."

We went in and Captain Hamner was quite civil. He said to the ladies, "Are you going to play four-balls?" The British usually play alternate shots. You play the same ball, hitting it alternately, and that's called a four-some. Four-balls is what we play in America 99 percent of the time. He looked out on the golf course and said, "Well, if you're gonna play a four-ball, I hope you won't dally around. I expect you to finish at least in three hours." It would normally take four hours in America.

We started off, and the girls were absolutely panicked. They were practically running trying to get around the golf course in three hour's time. They were muttering, "There's nobody on this damn golf course. Why are we being rushed so?"

I said, "Just do it. Get to your balls, and don't wait on protocol. Just hit the ball."

We got around the course in about three hours and 15 minutes. That's a pretty fast pace to play. When we came back to the club-house, Capt. Hamner greeted us. He said, "The grouse are absolutely wonderful, Mr. Harris. Why don't you and the ladies come into the Captain's Parlor?" This is a room where, supposedly, the ladies are never invited. We were invited into this inner sanctum, a lovely sitting room, and he said, "Do you like Scotch?"

I said, "Well, yes, I do."

It had been cool and we had not had lunch. It was around 2 p.m. He gave us a Muirfield measure. A Muirfield measure was somewhere between five and six ounces of straight Scotch in a goblet of sorts. I drank all of mine. Blessedly, my wife, Susie, did not drink all of hers, because by the time I got to the car, I was reeling, and she had to drive. We went to a little pub and had a sandwich, and Susie drove on to St. Andrews. We checked into the Old Course Hotel.

The next day, we went to the Royal & Ancient and were met by the captain, Keith McKinsey. Again, we'd been introduced by letter from the president of Pine Valley. Keith McKinsey was a legendary figure. The R&A is an imposing, prominent old stone building. It also has an inner sanctum where, supposedly, no women are allowed. But because of the special relationship of Pine Valley, Keith McKinsey took the women and us into the Trophy Room and to the main room, which looks out over the golf course. It was a special treat to see the trophies, everything earned by everybody who was anybody over many years on the old course. Hattie, George, Susie, and I played golf there. It was a windy day and quite remarkable things happened. I don't remember what I shot, but it was tolerable. Hattie Urschel had a caddie who disappeared behind a bush from time to time to get another nip of Scotch, and, by the time we finished playing, he could barely stagger home with the golf bag.

Almost every other green at the old course is a double green, servicing two holes. These greens were a hundred yards wide with undulations that were amazing, and they were very slick and fast. They had two flags on them—one for the hole you were playing and one for the hole that you would play coming back on the other nine holes. Dear Hattie, who had been club champion at Toledo Country Club years before, had a putt of at least 100 yards. She whacked that thing, and it went up and over and down and around the hills and the contours of the green and into the hole. It was the longest putt anybody could ever hit. I remind her of it every time I see her.

Dear memories of dear friends and wonderful places. That's golf.

L–R JERRY DIRVIN, FORMER EXEC VP PROCTOR AND GAMBLE,
FRANK HARRIS, DAN FERGUSON, FORMER CEO/CHAIRMAN
OF NEWELL-RUBBERMAID, BILL MCCARTNEY, OWNER OF
INDIUM CORP, PLAYING GOLF IN IRELAND AND SCOTLAND

DAN FERGUSON'S PERSONAL PLANE (NOT CORPORATE) WHICH WE
TOOK TO IRELAND, SCOTLAND AND ENGLAND. WHAT A WAY TO GO!

HOLE	1	2	3	4	5	6	7	8	9	OUT		10	11	12	13	14	15	16	17	18	IN	TOT	HCP NET
GOLD TEES	433	510	402	147	364	565	397	195	446	3459		412	364	510	177	388	577	405	184	442	3459	6918	
BLUE TEES	408	490	383	132	347	550	380	180	427	3297		378	331	457	157	368	555	372	163	427	3208	6505	
WHITE TEES	383	479	365	116	329	435	363	165	407	3042		344	331	457	137	350	437	338	138	372	2904	5946	
MEN'S HDCP	5	11	7	17	13	1	9	15	3			6	14	12	18	8	4	10	16	2			
PAR MEN'S / LADIES	4	5	4	3	4	5	4	3	4/5	36/37		4	4	5	3	4	5	4	3	4	36	72/73	
FRANK	5	6	③	②4	③	4	3	5		35		4	4	5	3	③	③	4	3	③	32	67	
2 Bogies					EAGLE											EAGLE							
9 PARS				June 2000 1st Time To shoot AGE																			
4 Birdies			OR Better																				
2 EAGLES			67 When I was 68 years old																				
			Played with Susie And Larry + Lyle Rankin																				
LADIES' HDCP	7	5	3	17	11	1	9	15	13			8	14	12	16	6	2	10	18	4			
RED TEES	333	404	365	116	329	435	363	165	407	2917		344	297	407	137	286	437	338	93	361	2700	5617	
RED/SILVER TEES	333	404	308	116	302	435	363	132	407	2800		259	297	407	117	238	437	295	93	361	2504	5304	

FIRST TIME TO SHOOT MY AGE OR BETTER, JUNE
2000. MY FINEST ROUND AS A SENIOR.

NTI

Working for a Safer World

Sam Nunn
Co-Chairman
Chief Executive Officer

January 19, 2007

Dear Frank:

   I had a great time being with you at the Naples Forum Club and on the golf course. Watching your great swing is going to help me in the future. In my view, the ultimate test of good company is having a poor round of golf and still having a good time. This test was met for me both days. I also had an unprecedented experience at the Port Royal seafood buffet, which has to be the world's best.

   I've taken the liberty of enclosing a few of my recent speeches and articles about our work at the Nuclear Threat Initiative. It is more information than you need, but I hope that you will find it of interest.

   Thanks again for your hospitality.

Sincerely,

Sam Nunn

Enclosures

Mr. Frank Harris
710 Buttonbush Lane
Naples, Florida 34i08

Nuclear Threat Initiative
1747 Pennsylvania Ave., NW
7th Floor
Washington, DC 20006
t 202.296.4810
f 202.296.4811
www.nti.org

A charitable organization working to reduce the global threat
from nuclear, biological and chemical weapons

LETTER FROM SAM NUNN SUBSEQUENT TO HIS VISIT
TO NAPLES AND SPEECH TO THE FORUM CLUB

33

Wealth and Posterity

Having spent 14 years with Owens-Illinois in a culture that did a great deal of entertaining at everything from golf, fishing, hunting, gin rummy, drinking, shows, and theater—all of the things that were done in a corporate world—I had a taste for the pleasure of doing that with customers. When I founded AIM Packaging and continued to generate and maintain sales, my wife and I probably didn't take a vacation for five or more years without having a customer in tow wherever we went, from Pebble Beach to the Bahamas to our home on Marco Island.

I have always felt that making money and having fun was the key to a successful and healthy life, as long as one did it in that order. I made speeches to my employees along the lines that if they weren't making any money, their jobs were in jeopardy, and if they weren't having any fun, their lives and health were in jeopardy. There has been no enforced servitude since the Civil War. A job is voluntary and if it isn't enjoyable should be exchanged for one that is.

Money is not very important unless you don't have any, and there have been times in my life when we had very little as my family struggled through the Depression and injuries and businesses that were not very productive. It put a real hunger in me to participate in the other side of the economic spectrum. From high school through college, I saw the delightful things that wealthy people enjoyed. I watched the wealthy people in Toledo, Ohio, who were friends of my wife's family. It was important to me to be as successful as I could. I had a lot of good advice. My father-in-law always advised me to "Keep chipping away at the old block," and "Don't get too impatient." The other side of that was a belief of a banker friend of mine who once said, "Hell, Frank, you're 30 some years old. *Carpe diem*, seize the day, get on with it. The first thing you know, you'll get comfortable in the level that you're at and won't be willing to take the risk." Chipping away at the old block fell by the wayside when I found the guts to take those risks, such as when I founded AIM Packaging.

When a person gets some money, there will be others like moths to a candle who want to help invest it. Care must be taken with how to invest money. I would certainly recommend to my children, grandchildren, and the great-grandchildren I probably will never meet, to be very careful with how they treat their money. Everyone needs to keep enough to have a safety net if things don't work out with risk capital, but shouldn't be afraid to go after risk capital, because that's the only way to experience the multiplier effect.

I've had wonderful experiences in the stock market were I invested $10 and got back $100. I've also had experiences where I invested $100 and got back $10. I had to balance those out and not get too discouraged with the latter case when I lost money. I had to continue to take those risks.

I also had to be prudent about studying what to do, or choose someone who was really good in the business and then watch them very carefully. I fired a lot of financial advisors because they did not perform well. They also got very rich disproportionately when they were playing with my chips. I had to be prepared to cut and run when they were not doing the job I felt they should. It's a good rule to not fall in love with your advisors. Keep them on guard to do well for you.

Taxes in this country are punitive. They penalize the most successful people. The redistribution of wealth is the essence of socialism, and that can be extended so far you can cause people to say, "Why should I work so hard when I have to give so much of the profits to the government?"

You have to keep that end balanced with the safety net that needs to be provided by Social Security. It was very important for my mother and father to have Social Security because they were not able to do better. I am sympathetic to that situation, but to continue to provide the entitlements that have been generated in this country is probably going to be its biggest hurdle. Also, it will be hard to preserve the incentive for people to make money.

Knowing the tax laws and being able to understand at least enough of them so that you protect your money for the present—and certainly for the future—has been something I studied well since accumulating a modest amount of money. I thought it was quite a lot of money until I moved to Naples and found that it was not very much at all compared with many people who move down there—super successful people, CEOs, executives, inheritors, or people who sold their businesses and cashed out for a pile of money and are down here living in a $20 million house.

As I have progressed through my 60s and 70s, I've made a lot of plans to shelter the wealth I've created and increase it with a lot of very complicated trust plans. We have revocable trusts, in case I need them. I can always tap them, but they facilitate passing on to the next generation with considerable shelters for taxes. There are businesses that we still have that have a considerable upside and generate a nice income. In 2004, I set up an irrevocable trust where we transferred 99 percent of the ownership of my current businesses to a trust for the benefit of my children and grandchildren. I kept 1 percent, which is the only vote. That allows me, if I need it, to take the money out, and it also allows me to pass that on at a time before the full maturity of an income stream is complete.

In the land developing business, in which we've got a considerable amount, I don't get my money out of the front end. It comes out way down the road, and, quite frankly, our projections that we'd do this within five to eight years were considerably erroneous. It's taken over 20 years for it to begin to kick out.

You have to be prepared for the best and the worst. It's hard to see unexpected bumps in the road like the S&L debacle of the '80s, the

banking and construction industry going down the tube in the early
'90s, and the market dropping off the wall in 2000.

We have taken all these steps to continue to enjoy the lifestyle that
a reasonable amount of money has provided. But we also want to provide for our children and grandchildren with a safety net for education and reasonable comfort. But it will come with restrictions. We
don't want some wastrel acting as if he doesn't have to do anything.
We have many, many pages of covenants to prevent trust fund babies
from being useless.

34

Our Children

S usie and I have two children of whom we are very proud. Our
first child is Virginia Draper Harris, born September 6, 1958. We
call her Gingi. In spite of an encephalitis attack that hospitalized
her in Baltimore when she was four, she made a complete recovery
and had a normal childhood. She was particularly athletic in her high
school years—outstanding on the trampoline.

L-R BECKY, WALTER, FRANK, SUSIE, GINGI

L-R GINGI, FRANK, SUSIE, WALTER

GINGI, ADDY AND SUSIE IN OUR MAUMEE HOME

GRANDDAUGHTER
ADDY ROTHMAN AT
16 YEARS OF AGE

GRANDSON SAM
ROTHMAN AT 14
YEARS OF AGE

Gingi went to Endicott College in Beverly, Massachusetts, for two years and then to Skidmore College in Saratoga Springs, New York, majoring in early childhood education. She worked in New York City for the Atlantic Monthly for five years in advertising and special events. After marriage to Josh Rothman, whom she had known in high school, the newlyweds returned to Toledo, where they both worked for me at Green Cove Development Corporation. They were married for 14 years before calling it quits, but not before providing us with two wonderful grandchildren.

Gingi is now a teacher in Maumee Valley Country Day School, and her two children are students there. We're very proud of our grandchildren—Virginia Adair Rothman, 16, and Samuel Harris Rothman, 14. They have their own home. Gingi is not remarried at this point. She's 48 years old and very attractive. She's a down-to-earth soccer mom and also a good mother and teacher.

DAUGHTER GINGI AS A TEACHER
AND "SOCCER MOM," 2006

Our son, Walter Corlett Harris, was born December 2, 1960 in Baltimore. He was one of the cutest kids ever while he was growing up. He's still a very handsome man at 46 years old. He had a normal childhood, was a fair student through public school, and then transferred to Maumee Valley Country Day School for high school. He and I have enjoyed many good times playing golf, tennis, hunting, and fishing. When he was in high school, he and I fished for salmon in Quebec. We also did a lot of bird hunting together as he grew up.

SON WALTER WITH
A GROUPER ON
MARCO ISLAND

WALTER WITH A
PHEASANT IN OHIO

After high school, Walter attended the University of Richmond in Richmond, Virginia, for two years. He then decided to transfer to the University of North Carolina—my alma mater. I was very pleased with that. An undergraduate degree there in business administration was followed by two years in the business world and then an MBA back at the university. At that time, I was on the board of the Institute of Private Enterprise at UNC and was there several times as executive in residence. I was actually teaching in one of my son's classes. That was quite rewarding.

L-R FRANK, SUSIE, JENNIFER, WALTER, GINGI
AND JOSH. IN FRONT SAM AND ADDY

Walter is married to Jennifer Kulzak, a beautiful, bright woman who graduated from Miami University, Oxford, Ohio. She was a cheerleader there and is always most pleasant company. Jennifer was born in Toledo, Ohio on March 12, 1970. After graduation she worked for then Governor George Voinovich for four years and then a year in Republican fundraising for Voinovich, Senator DeWine, and Senator Dole among others. She left fundraising and taught for four years. Jennifer and Walter have two terrific sons—Welles Francis Harris and Grant Corlett Harris. Their home is in Gates Mills, Ohio. Walter has much experience in business, which will serve him well.

JENNIFER K. HARRIS,
SON WALTER'S WIFE

JENNIFER AND
WALTER AT
REHEARSAL
DINNER THE
NIGHT BEFORE
THEY MARRIED

L-R GRANDSONS GRANT C. HARRIS (5) AND WELLES
F. HARRIS (7), WALTER AND JENNIFER'S SONS

Susie and I are obviously very proud of our children and grandchildren. We enjoy their visits wherever we may be, whether Florida, Ohio, or Michigan.

FAMILY
PICTURE
CIRCA 1996

Epilogue

Well, the job is done. If you are reading this you have a copy of my memoirs. On several occasions I've referred to this as an ego trip and it probably is. But it's more than just an ego trip. It's therapy!

Writing this book has caused me to reflect on and ponder events in my life that I hadn't thought about in a long time. When you think about where you came from and then where you are today, the question that begs to be answered is: How did that happen? Was it luck? Talent? Brilliance? Circumstances?

As I write this I'm in my 75th year. That particular milestone will come up soon enough on January 15, 2008. Age gives one a good perspective to view the past and try to answer the question of how it happened. Looking back I can identify three powerful forces that propelled me to where I am today and I've alluded to these in this book.

First, growing up in the small town of Lincolnton, North Carolina I had the great fortune of experiencing the work ethic from an early age. Farm chores and working in my dad's gas station were as natural and as expected as saying "Yes, sir" and "Yes, mam." We weren't exactly poor but there was a degree of economic uncertainty during those depression and war years. At the same time I could see how the mill owners and other highly successful families were living. That served to whet my appetite for all the fun things in life that wealth could provide.

Second, being able to play golf at a competitive level has been both a confidence builder and avenue to important friendships. The job just out of college with Owens-Illinois was due to a golf conversation. As

I was building AIM Packaging many more sales were made on the golf course than in a business suit. And I think golf is a character builder. The game teaches so many characteristics such as patience, determination and self discipline. The camaraderie found in golf is just special for relaxation and building bonds of trust and friendship—essential to success.

And third, I married the right woman. I dedicated this book to Susie because she always believed in me, even when I was very unsure of what to do next. Through the over fifty years of marriage we have become a team. Susie has a calm resolve and perceptive intuition that has made her my most valuable asset. She is my soul mate and I will always be glad I had the good sense to call her for that second date many years ago.

Those are the three important elements that led me to where I am today. But when all is said and done there is an element inside each of us that must be met and satisfied. As we live our lives, making decisions and taking actions, there is a judge rendering opinions along the way. Those opinions weigh in the balance and tip either toward positive or negative self-esteem. To act with confidence and be successful you must have positive self-esteem.

I will end this Epilogue with the following poem which captures so well the "judge" who must be satisfied.

The Guy in the Glass
by Dale Wimbrow, (c) 1934

When you get what you want in your struggle for self,
And the world makes you King for a day,
Then go to the mirror and look at yourself,
And see what that guy has to say.
For it isn't your Father, or Mother, or Wife,
Who judgment upon you must pass.
The feller whose verdict counts most in your life
Is the guy staring back from the glass.

He's the feller to please, never mind all the rest,
For he's with you clear up to the end,
And you've passed your most dangerous, difficult test
If the guy in the glass is your friend.
You may be like Jack Horner and "chisel" a plum,
And think you're a wonderful guy,
But the man in the glass says you're only a bum
If you can't look him straight in the eye.
You can fool the whole world down the pathway of years,
And get pats on the back as you pass,
But your final reward will be heartaches and tears
If you've cheated the guy in the glass.

Appendices

Appendix A

Documentation of Susie's membership in The National Society of the Colonial Dames of America

---

WILLIAM LEETE

Ancestor of:
Virginia D. Harris and Donna D. Burr

So many Puritans flocked to the Connecticut Valley in 1635 that that year is considered by many to be the official date for the beginning of the colony.

After swearing oaths of loyalty etc,. any householder could go to the town meeting but only "Freemen", those of prominence and substance who were decided upon by a magistrate or the general court, could vote. Less than one-third were Freemen. Freemen were elected deputies to the general court which chose the magistrates - one of whom was selected governor.

In the beginning, New Haven was not connected to the Connecticut Colony. New Haven was settled by Puritans from London who hoped to have a center for commerce. When that did not work out, they turned to agriculture, but the area was not very well suited to farming. It was an extreme Puritan community, unlike Connecticut Colony. In New Haven Colony, the Freemen had to be church members and a select group of them formed the General Court. It was also unique in that it did not allow trial by jury.

The Connecticut Colony was formed by the joining together of several communities; Hartford, Winsor and Weathersfield. The New Haven Colony was formed the same way in 1643 with the town of New Haven joining with Milford, Guilford, Stamford, Southland (on Long Island) and Branford. It was a loose confederation with New Haven the dominant town. This was made necessary in 1643 by the organization of a group who called themselves the New England Confederation. It was formed for "mutual safety and welfare" by representatives of the colonies of Massachusetts Bay, Plymouth, Connecticut and New Haven. Primarily it was formed for defense. In 1675-76, it undertook its most important task — breaking the power of the Southern New England Indians in King Philips War. The Confederation was dissolved in 1684.

As colonies, Connecticut and New Haven had no standing in England until 1662. At that time Connecticut secured a legal charter and acquired the New Haven colony in the process.

William Leete

It was mainly during this period that William Leete lived and, I believe, we can safely assume he was a Puritan. He was born in England in 1612, but he lived in the Connecticut area from age seventeen in 1639 to 1683 when he died April 11th in Hartford, Connecticut. He was married to Anna Payne who, I believe, was born in 1613 and died in 1668.

At the age of 41, William Leete became a Magistrate of New Haven Colony. From 1653-1658 he held that position; then from 1658-1660 he was the Deputy Governor of New Haven Colony and Governor from 1661-1664. He was Commissioner of the United Colonies from New Haven from 1664-1665, 1666,1667,1668, 1672, 1675, 1678 and was President of the Board in 1667, 1673 and 1678. The record shows that he was Assistant of Connecticut (whatever that is) from 1665-1668.

(1)

SUPPORTING NARRATIVE FOR SUSIE'S MEMBERSHIP
IN THE NATIONAL SOCIETY OF THE COLONIAL DAMES
OF AMERICA (CONTINUED ON NEXT 3 PAGES)

He was also Commissioner to Rhode Island in 1668, 1670 and 1671. In 1668, he became Deputy Governor of Connecticut and remained in that post through 1675. He became Governor in 1676 at the age of 64 and was governor of the Connecticut Colony for **six years** through 1682. William Leete died the following year at age 70.

John Leete

The line continues through John Leete, **the son of William** Leete and Anna Payne. John Leete was born in 1639 and died in 1692. The record shows he lived in Guilford, Connecticut. He married Mary Chittenden who was born in 1647 and died in 1692.

Anna Leete

John and Mary Leete's daughter Anna was born in 1671 and died in 1724. She **was married to John Collins** who was born in 1665(?) in Guilford, Connecticut **and died in 1751 in Guilford.**

Avis Collins

Avis Collins was the daughter of Anna and John Collins. She **was born in** Guilford in 1714 and died in 1754 in Litchfield, Connecticut. On December 26, 1734 Avis married Peter Buell, Sr. who was born in Lebanon, Connecticut in 1710 and died in Litchfield, Connecticut in 1784. Peter Buell, Sr. was the grandson of Samuel Buell who was a deputy from Killingworth to the General Court of Connecticut and the great-grandson of Edward Griswold who was also a deputy to the Connecticut General Court from Winsor and later from Killingworth.

Peter Buell, Jr.

Born on October 12, 1739 in Litchfield, Connecticut and died on Jan 30, 1797, Peter Buell, Jr. was the son of Avis Collins and Peter Buell, Sr. He married Abigail Seymour December 25, 1766 in Litchfield. Abigail was born in 1746 and died in 1806.

Abigail Buell

Abigail Buell, daughter of Peter Buell, Jr. and Abigail Seymour was born May 3, 1770 in Litchfield, Connecticut and died October 27, 1847 in Litchfield. She married Melanchthon Woolsey Welles in Litchfield on February 7, 1794. He was born December 6, 1770 in Stamford, Connecticut and died in 1857. His parents were the Reverend Noah Welles and Abigail Woolsey Welles.

Melanchthon Woolsey Welles

Melanchthon Woolsey Welles, known as Woolsey, possibly **was born in Lanesboro,** Massachusetts on May 26, 1802. However, another source says he was born in Ohio. His parents were Abigail and Melanchton Woolsey Welles. He was admitted to the bar in 1823 and was a lawyer and prosecuting attorney in Cleveland and Elyria, Ohio. For a year he was a collector of tolls and postmaster in Akron, Ohio; a

(2)

justice of the peace in Akron for four and a half years, and then traveled the State as an agent of the Ohio State Temperance Society for about one year. He then returned to the practice of law in Elyria and Cleveland. As a lawyer, he was not very successful. Apparently this was due to his vociferous anti-slavery position. His home was a stop on the underground railway. About 1850, he was appointed agent of the state for the Sale of Western Reserve School Lands and moved to Defiance, Ohio. In 1858, he moved to Fort Dodge, Iowa. According to one source he went because he was appointed to an Iowa land agency. Another source says he went in the interest of his brother, William B. Welles, who was one of the owners of Des Moines River Lands. While there, he also practiced law. He owned lime stone quarries in Fort Dodge and his heirs and descendants through my mother's generation received a small income from them. (Currently a Fort Dodge descendant is trying to trace all heirs and recipiants of bequests (ie. churches) to get their consent to the sale of these worked-out quarries to the county for a landfill.)

Woolsey Welles was married twice and had two children by Mary W. Brown his first wife. They were married in 1829 and she died in 1836. He had seven or eight children by Zilpha Long Henderson, his second wife. They were married December 21, 1836 at Elyria, Ohio. Zilpha was born in 1818 in Hatfield, MA., and died March 17, 1882 in Fort Dodge, Iowa. The fourth and fifth children of Woolsey Welles were twins - William B. Welles and George E. Welles. (William B. is David Welles' grandfather and George E. is my great-grandfather.) Woolsey Welles died November 16, 1896 in Fort Dodge, Iowa.

George E. Welles

George E. Welles was born July 4, 1840 in either Cleveland or Elyria, Ohio and moved to Toledo in 1859. He worked as a clerk in the wholesale house of West and Traux. On April 14, 1861, he enlisted as a private in Company E of the Fourteenth Ohio Volunteers which was being organized at that time. In January 1862 his regiment joined General Grant's army which was then operating on the Cumberland River in Tennessee. He rose through the ranks quickly and in 1865 was given a full commission as a Colonel. On the 16th of March 1865, shortly before the end of the war, he was brevetted Brigadier General for "gallant and meritorious conduct". He was known as the "boy Colonel" throughout the army of the Tennessee. His division commander, Major General Leggett, said of him "That boy never made a mistake." He and his regiment went through some of the "hottest" fighting and longest battles of the war - from the Tennessee and Cumberland Rivers, Shiloh, Vicksburg, and Chattanooga to Atlanta. From Atlanta, they went with Sherman to the sea, then on from Savannah to the Carolinas. They were part of Sherman's army present as the last main part of the Confederate Army under Joseph E. Johnston Surrendered. George E. Welles led his regiment in the Grand Review in Washington D.C. and then they proceeded to Louisville, KY where on July 10, 1865 they disbanded. He made a touching speech to his men at that time and they presented him with a dress sabre.

General Welles returned to Toledo. He became assistant Postmaster and was also in the grain business. President Grant appointed him assessor of internal revenue which he remained until the post was discontinued. From 1887-1894 he was in Deluth, MN as Secretary of the Board of Trade. When he returned to Toledo he

(3)

represented the New York Life Insurance Company. He was also deputy county clerk
under two administrations. Ill health forced him to retire from public
life in 1903 and he died April 27, 1906. George E. Welles was married to
Julia Elliot Smith in Toledo on May 24, 1877. She was born in Toledo on
June 21, 1851 and died there November 26, 1911. Julia was the daughter of
Julia Ellen Hunt and Denison B. Smith and the granddaughter of John Elliot Hunt.
John E. Hunt was the first white settler and trader in the Maumee, Ohio area
and later a prominent citizen of Maumee. George E. Welles and Julia Smith had
two boys, William B. Welles and George D. Welles, my grandfather.

George Denison Welles

George D. Welles, the younger son of George E. and Julia Welles, was born on
November 21, 1881 in Toledo and died there December 30, 1948. On September 11, 1907
he married Mae Elizabeth Hunker. She was born January 10, 1882 in Chicago, IL,
but her family moved to Toledo when she was a child. She died in Toledo on
March 30, 1972. They had two children George Denison Welles, Jr. and Margaret
Virginia Welles.

George D. Welles attended sessions at the law department of the University of
Michigan and studied in the law office of King and Tracy in Toledo. He was
admitted to the bar in 1903 and later was admitted to practice in all the
U.S. Courts. He stayed with King and Tracy until 1908 when he bacame a partner in
the firm of King, Tracy, Chapman and Welles - which in 1914 became Tracy, Chapman
and Welles. In 1921, he received an honorary law degree from the University of
Michigan. He became head of the law firm which then bore the name of Welles,
Kelsey, Coburn, Fuller and Harrington. He defended Owens-Illinois in the anti-
trust suits brought against them by the federal government and commuted to
Washington D.C. He was very active in many community activities and prominent
in the legal community of Toledo. He used to go by boat, a Dart, from his summer
home in Maumee to his office in downtown Toledo. The chauffeur would drop him
off there and pick him up at the end of the day.

Margaret Virginia Welles

Margaret Virginia Welles, known as Tookie, was born in Toledo October 15, 1910.
Her family lived on Collins Street. When she was ten, they moved to Collingwood
Avenue between Bancroft and Virginia. In the summer, the family moved to "the
country" on the river in Maumee. She attended the Misses Smead's School in Toledo
and Miss Hartridge's School in Plainfield, NJ. Tookie attended Smith College and
on May 14, 1930 married William Corlett Draper "Biggie" of Toledo. She was
active in the Junior League of Toledo, the American Red Cross and various other
community activities in Toledo. They had two daughters, Virginia Welles Draper,
born March 2, 1933 and Donna Adair Draper, born March 21, 1935.

Tookie died in Toledo on June 25, 1967. Biggie died March 8, 1974 also in Toledo.
He had worked for the Toledo Trust Company for most of his adult life - establishing
the Trust Department there and heading it throughout his career.

(4)

Virginia Welles Draper

Virginia Welles Draper, always known as "Susie", was born March 2, 1933 in
Flower Hospital Toledo. She attended Fulton School and graduated from Maumee
Valley Country Day School and Vassar College. She worked for McGraw-Hill
Publishing Company in New York City and North Shore Country Day School in
Winnetka, IL. On September 29, 1956, in St. Paul's Episcopal Church in Maumee,
she married Francis Meetze Harris ("Frank") who was born in Lincolnton, NC on
January 15, 1933 and who graduated from the University of North Carolina.

They have two children Virginia Draper Harris ("Gingi") and Walter Corlett Harris.
Gingi was born in Toledo, also in Flower Hospital, on September 6, 1958, and
married Joshua Damon Rothman on September 6, 1986. Walter was born in Baltimore,
Maryland on December 2, 1960 and was married to Debra Anne Gifford, July 7, 1990.

(5)

The National Society of The Colonial Dames of America

in

The State of Connecticut

Mrs. Francis Meetze Harris

Full Maiden Name... Virginia Welles Draper

Full Address... 1714 River Road

Maumee, Ohio

PRESENTS PROOF OF ELIGIBILITY IN RIGHT OF DESCENT FROM

............William Leete............
[Name of ancestor from whom eligibility is derived.]

who was born in.....England............................on.....1612..............................
[Town, City, or County.]

was a resident of...Guilford, Connecticut............and died in...Hartford, Connecticut............
[Town, City, or County.]   [Town, City, or County.]

on.....April 16, 1683..................... The principal service upon which my claim of eligibility to membership

is based, is as follows: Governor, Connecticut Colony, 1676-1682.

Proof of this service:

Public Records of Connecticut 1665-   p. 273, etc.

Register of Ancestors   NSCDA in the State of Connecticut p.32

_____   _____
Colonial State President   Associate State President

No. 761

Associate State.... Ohio

No. 1958

Colonial State.... Connecticut

GENEALOGY SUPPORTING SUSIE'S MEMBERSHIP IN
NSCDA (CONTINUED ON NEXT 5 PAGES)

Colonial State...... Connecticut .... No...1958

Associate State...... Ohio .... No......

Full Maiden Name: **1. Generation.** (Candidate)   Town or City

Virginia Welles Draper............ born... March 2, 1933 ... in ...Toledo, Ohio........

a legal resident of... Maumee, Ohio .... wife of ...Francis Meetze Harris ....who was

born. January 15, 1933 .... in ...Lincolnton, North Carolina........

died.. in......................................

date married (1, 2, 3)...September 29, 1956................ in...Maumee, Ohio..............

References:

2 Birth Certificates
Marriage License

2. Generation.

William Corlett Draper............... b. November 20, 1904... in ...Toledo, Ohio.............

                                   d... March 8, 1974 ..... in ... Toledo, Ohio ....

Margaret Virginia Welles................ b... October 15, 1910... in ...Toledo, Ohio.............

                                   d... July 25, 1967.......... in ...Toledo, Ohio.............

              date married (1, 2, 3)... May 14, 1932 .... in ... Toledo, Ohio ....

References:

Birth Certificates
Marriage License
Death Certificates

3. Generation.

George Denison Welles............ b. November 21, 1881... in ...Toledo, Ohio.................

                                d... December 30, 1948 ,, in ... Toledo, Ohio ....

Mae Elizabeth Hunker........................ b... January 10, 1882... in ...Chicago, Illinois........

                                d... March 30, 1972 ... in ... Toledo, Ohio ....

              date married (1, 2, 3)...September 11, 1907n ...Toledo, Ohio....................

References:

   1900 Census Toledo, Ohio Lucas County
   Birth Certificates- Death Certificates
   Marriage License

Mrs./Miss....Francis M. Harris................   Colonial State...Connecticut............ No..1958...

Associate State....Ohio............................. No...................

4. Generation.

...George E. Welles..............................   b..July 4, 1840........ in..Cleveland, Ohio..............

d..April 27, 1906........ in..Toledo, Ohio..............

...Julia Elliott Smith.........................   b...June 20, 1851.... in..Toledo, Ohio..............

d..November 26, 1911.. in ..Toledo, Ohio..............

date married (1, 2, 3)..May 24, 1877........... in ..Toledo, Ohio..............

References:

1900 Census-Toledo, Ohio Lucas County

Lucas County, Ohio Death Certificates

5. Generation.

...Melancthon "Woolsey"Welles.......... b...May 26, 1802............. in ..Lanesboro, Massachusetts

d.....1896............................ in ....

...Zilpha Long Henderson.................. b.......1818...................... in ..Hatfield, Massachusetts

d...March 17, 1882..... in ..Ft. Dodge, Iowa............

date married (1, 2, 3)..December 21, 1836 in ....Elyria, Ohio..................

References:

1850 Census, Defiance, Ohio   1880 Census Fort Dodge, Iowa

Marriage Records, Lorain Co. Ohio 1824-1848 Vol. I

6. Generation.

...Melancthon Woolsey Welles.......... b...December 6, 1770.. in Stamford, Connecticut

d.............1857................ in ....

Abigail Buell   b..May 3, 1770......... in ..Litchfield, Connecticut

d...October 27, 1847... in ..Litchfield, Connecticut

date married (1, 2, 3)..February 7, 1794.. in ....

References:

Barbour Collection, Connecticut Vital Records Reel 75

Vital Records Litchfield, Conn. Vol. I, p. 43

Buell Genealogy, Albert Welles p. 87, 202

Mrs./Miss Francis Meetze Harris

Colonial State Connecticut   No. 1958

Associate State Ohio   No.

7. Generation.

Peter Buell, Jr.

b October 12, 1739 in Litchfield, Connecticut

d January 30, 1797 in Litchfield, Connecticut

Abigail Seymour

b April 4, 1746 in Harwinton, Connecticut

d May 16, 1806 in Litchfield, Connecticut

date married (1, 2, 3) December 25, 1766 in Litchfield, Connecticut

References:

Vital Records I p. 86 Litchfield, Connecticut also p. 43
Buell Genealogy p. 52

8. Generation.

Peter Buell, Sr.

b May 22, 1710 in Lebanon, Connecticut

d May 10, 1784 in Litchfield, Connecticut

Avis Collins

b April 1, 1714 in Guilford, Connecticut

d November 1, 1754 in Litchfield, Connecticut

date married (1, 2, 3) December 26, 1734 in Litchfield, Connecticut

References:

Buell Genealogy pp. 51,52

9. Generation.

John Collins

b 1665-70 in Guilford, Connecticut

d January 24, 1751 in

Anna Leete

b August 5, 1671 in

d November 2, 1724 in

date married (1, 2, 3) July 23, 1691 in

References:

The Descendants of William Leete compiled by Edward L. Leete
Guilford, Conn. 1884 2nd. edition 1934 New Haven page 3

10 **Generation.**

John Leete .... b .... 1639 .... in Guilford, Connecticut
d November 25, 1692 in Guilford, Connecticut
Mary Chittenden .... b .... 1647 .... in ....
d March 19, 1712 in ....
date married (1, 2, 3) October 4, 1670 in ....
References:

Leete Genealogy p. 1

11 **Generation.**

William Leete .... b .... 1613 .... in Dodington, England
d April 16, 1683 in Hartford, Connecticut
Anna Payne .... b .... 1613? .... in ....
d September 1, 1668 in ....
date married (1, 2, 3) August 1, 1636 in Hail-Weston, England
References:

Leete Genealogy p. 1

Mrs./Miss.. Francis Meetze Harris

FAMILY DATA

Parents of candidate's husband { Name of father.... Walter Lee Harris
{ Maiden name of mother... Marbell Meetze

Children of candidate (Note if by adoption):

Name	Date of Birth	Place of Birth	Name of husband/wife
Virginia Draper Harris	Sept. 6, 1958	Toledo, Ohio	-------
Walter Corlett Harris	Dec. 2, 1960	Baltimore, Md.	-------

If the data in this form was compiled by other than the candidate, please sign:

....
Name   Address   Date
....

AFFIDAVIT

I declare upon my honor that the facts herein set forth are true to the best of my knowledge and belief.
Also, that if admitted to membership of this State Society I shall comply with its Constitution and By-Laws, with the Constitution and By-Laws of The National Society of The Colonial Dames of America, and I will always support the Constitution of The United States of America.

Subscribed and sworn to before me this.... 11TH .... Virginia D. Harris
(Signature of Candidate)

day of.... May 19 86

Virginia D. Smith

LOREN C. SENGSTOCK, Lucas County
Notary Public, State of Ohio
My commission expires August 31, 1983

Mrs. Anderton Lewis Bentley, JR.   Mrs. William R. Crawford
Proposer   Seconder(s)

I have examined and approved the references herein or photo copies thereof.

Ruth L. Harlow   June 2, 1980
Verifying Genealogist   Date

No. 1958 .... Connecticut ....   September 8, 1980
                        Colonial State   Date Approved by Colonial State Society

No. .... Ohio   Lucy E. Holcombe
                        Associate State   Colonial State Registrar
                                                 Assistant Registrar

Appendix B

*In 1991 I was encouraged to apply for the position of Dean
of the Kenan-Flagler Business School, UNC-Chapel Hill.
The following documents relate to that process.*

THE UNIVERSITY OF NORTH CAROLINA
AT
CHAPEL HILL

SCHOOL OF JOURNALISM
AND MASS COMMUNICATION
Office of the Dean

Tel: (919) 962-1204
Fax: (919) 962-0620

The University of North Carolina at Chapel Hill
Campus Box 3365, Howell Hall
Chapel Hill, NC 27599-3365

October 31, 1991

Mr. Francis M. Harris
Green Cove
8781 West State Route 2
Oak Harbor, OH 43449

Dear Mr. Harris:

You have been suggested as an outstanding potential
applicant for the deanship of the Kenan-Flagler Business
School of the University of North Carolina at Chapel Hill.

You may know that Paul Rizzo, the current dean, decided
not to seek reappointment to a second term. His current
term ends June 30, 1992, and we hope to have a successor
named to succeed him effective July 1, 1992.

The Kenan-Flagler Business School has great momentum
now, with a number of important projects and international
activities under way. The splendid Kenan Center and Kenan
Institute are part of the Business School, of course, and a
handsome new Business School building is in the planning.

We are conducting a national search open to both
academics and professionals. Ads are appearing in national
and international publications, and notices are being sent
to all accredited business schools in the United States.
But we are going beyond the usual advertising and publicity,
and that's the reason for this letter to you.

If you are interested in being considered for the
position, please apply. A copy of the job description is
enclosed.

The search committee -- a group of 16 people, mostly
from the Business School but with representatives from the
greater University and from the professional business
community -- has a short time frame. We will begin

I WAS HONORED TO BE NOMINATED FOR THE DEANSHIP OF THE
KENAN-FLAGLER BUSINESS SCHOOL OF THE UNIVERSITY OF NORTH
CAROLINA AT CHAPEL HILL (CONTINUED ON NEXT 4 PAGES).

reviewing applications on November 15 and hope to interview
the semifinalists in January. Our chancellor has asked that
we give him our slate of finalists by the end of February.

Very best wishes.

Sincerely,

Richard Cole
Dean, School of Journalism
and Mass Communication and
Chairman of the Search
Committee

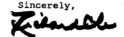

CONDOMINIUM RESORT

November 11, 1991

Dean Richard Cole
Search Committee Chairman
for Dean of the Kenan-Flagler Business School
Campus Box 3365, Howell Hall
U.N.C.
Chapel Hill, NC 27599-3365

Dear Dean Cole:

I am highly honored to have been asked to apply for this position. Thank you
for the compliment.

As a Trustee of the Kenan Institute for Private Enterprise for the past five years,
I've come to know many of the leaders of the University for whom I feel great
admiration. Also by participating in discussions with major university players
such as Bill Friday, Paul Hardin, Paul Rizzo, Jack Kasarda, Bob Eubanks and
Frank Kenan, to drop a few names, I have come to appreciate the value to society
of the goals being set by these great contributors and the joy of their achievements.

I'm aware of the frustrations facing any self-proclaimed mover and shaker and while
I won't pretend to relish such impediments, I guess I've matured enough by now to
regard the process as part of the game. Defining and refining a program through
consensus-making efforts are just part of the price of progressive change.

I consider myself first and foremost a salesman and an entrepreneur. The enjoyment
of taking an idea (anybody's good idea) and molding it into presentation form, then
making the pitch with great back-up stats and a little show biz, then "getting the
order"; it's just like winning a Pulitzer Prize!

For the last thirty years I've been President/CEO or Chairman of successful businesses
most of which I founded or cofounded (sometimes confounded). I've been elected to
industry association chairmanships and have worked with committees, congress and
bureaus from E.P.A. and F.D.A. to Fish & Wildlife.

I've worked with, and am friends with, top management people in the consumer
packaging insustries, ie. Proctor and Gamble, Bristol Meyers; the petrochemical
industries, glass, paper and plastic industries and now the construction and resort
development business.

I know investment bankers nationally and internationally, and have had the Dean of
Stanford's business school (Rene McPherson), and a prominent economist (Gary Shilling)
on the Board of my private company (Aim Packaging Inc.) among many other high level
contacts/friends.

GREEN COVE CONDOMINIUM RESORT   GREEN COVE DEVELOPMENT CORPORATION
8781 W. STATE ROUTE 2, OAK HARBOR, OHIO 43449   **(419) 898-3398**

I was a member of the Young Presidents Organization at age 38, a member of the World Business Council at age 49, and an active member of The Chief Executive Organization (10% of Y.P.O. are invited to join.)

My wife and I have travelled the world, love the people and art of the world, have played golf, fished and hunted birds on five continents. We play most of the games well from racket sports to wine tasting. Our family is very close, well-educated and reasonably successful - We're very lucky!

Now, if you're tired of reading how terrific my life has been (is), I'm a little sick of telling it.

So why am I applying for this job? We have enough money (I think), more friends and playmates than we can service, more toys than we can use, etc.

I guess the public service itch is part ethic and part ego driven. The desire to do something else with intelligent people has great appeal.

I have loved the experience of being executive in residence a couple of times at U.N.C. and at Bowling Green University. Spending time with these wonderful young people has been great fun - It certainly beats playing golf or sitting around with successful old crocks at elite clubs taking turns telling about the past and how screwed up the world is becoming.

When I got my golf handicap down to 3 this year and won 2 club championships and 5 member-guest tournements, I discovered no one really cared.

When we got back from a month in Italy this fall - from a museum tour - I realized that a steady diet of that wasn't my bag. I could beg for bucks under many worthy banners or I could throw myself full time into the businesses I own, and with the state of the economy maybe I should.

Now with all these thoughts being current contemplative considerations --- up pops your offer to apply for the deanship of Kenan-Flagler. The deanship wow! I wish mother were alive. The offer alone would have made her so proud!

If you choose to persue this further through interviews, I'm sure you know what you want in a dean. If you're searching for pomp and prestige as prerequisites, then please consider me no more. If you want a pragmatic, somewhat irreverent simplifier, who regards a sinecure as sinful, and humor as helpful then maybe we should talk. I like the programs and progress Dean Rizzo and his team have started and I would try mightily to make a positive difference while conserving the established greatness of the school.

I hate most resumes, (I've read thousands) they are usually just vanity valves and I'm not sure this one's any better, but thank you for reading it. I hope it will give some facts and flavor about the author.

Sincerely,

Francis M. Harris

```
                   BIOGRAPHICAL SKETCH FOR MR. FRANCIS M. HARRIS

    Address:       227 Polynesia Ct.           Summer:  1714 River Rd.
                   Marco Island, FL  33937               Maumee, OH  43537
                   (813) 394-6332                        (419) 893-9443

    Business:      Green Cove Development Corp.
                   8781 W. State Route 2
                   Oak Harbor, OH  43449
                   (419) 898-3398
                   (419) 8982698 - fax

    Birth Place: Lincolnton, NC

    Education:     B.S. University North Carolina - Chapel Hill 1955
                   Harvard - Advanced Business Course
                   Continuing Education through Y.P.O. and C.E.O. seminars

    Business:      Owens-Illinois, marketing 15 years
                   Aim Packaging Inc., founder 1969-1989 (sold '89)*
                   Green Cove Development Corp., founder 1986- *
                   Wild Wings Inc., founder 1986- *
                   Frank Harris and Associates Inc., founder 1988- *
                   * C.E.O. of above and principal owner.

    Board          Kenan Institute of Private Enterprise - Chapel Hill
    Membership:    Plastic Technologies Inc., Toledo, Ohio
                   Brazeway Inc., Adrian, MI

    Associations:  Chief Executive Organization
                   World Business Council
                   Young Presidents Organization (former)
                   Plastic Pioneers

    Clubs:         Belmont, Pine Valley, Royal Poinciana, Hole-in-the-Wall, Wilderness
                   Eagle Creek

    Activities:    Golf, Tennis, Hunting, Fishing, and Travel

    Status:        Happily married 35 years to Virginia (Susie) Draper - Vassar '55
                   Daughter - Virginia H. Rothman - Skidmore '80
                   Son - Walter C. Harris - UNC '83, UNC/MBA '87
                   Granddaughter - Virginia Adair Rothman - UNC 2013
```

THE UNIVERSITY OF NORTH CAROLINA
AT
CHAPEL HILL

SCHOOL OF JOURNALISM
AND MASS COMMUNICATION
Office of the Dean

Tel: (919) 962-1204
Fax: (919) 962-0620

The University of North Carolina at Chapel Hill
Campus Box 3365, Howell Hall
Chapel Hill, NC 27599-3365

November 14, 1991

Mr. Francis M. Harris
Green Cove
8781 W. State Route 2
Oak Harbor, OH 43449

Dear Mr. Harris:

Thank you for applying for the deanship of the Kenan-Flagler School of Business at the University of North Carolina at Chapel Hill.

The search committee is charged with finding the best-qualified person to fill this vital position. The scope of the search includes both the business and academic communities.

The search committee will review your résumé thoroughly and keep it in strict confidence. We hope to issue invitations in early December to a small number of semifinalists to come to our campus for interviews in January.

We are committed to the challenge of finding the right person to serve as the next dean of the Business School. We sincerely appreciate your interest in the position.

Very best wishes.

Cordially,

Richard Cole
Dean and Chairman of
the Search Committee

You write a great letter. Your credentials are excellent, and you'll be hearing from us again. Very best regards.

Appendix C

Letter from Robert O. Ebert, Chairman and
Co-Founder AIM Packaging, Inc.

I remember well the day Jack Harris brought his brother, Frank, to visit at my office. Jack thought we had a lot in common—we both liked plastics, fishing, hunting and golf.

After an hour or so we did find that we did have a lot in common—more than we ever realized at the time.

Frank invited me to join their Toledo hunting group for geese and duck on the Chesapeake. Being a field hunter, I knew little of water bird hunting. I did know it would be cold, so I took boots, a heavy insulated safety yellow coat and pants. To "quiet" the outfit down, I took a light weight dove hunting camouflaged slip over. By the second day, after the gang got to know me, we had many jokes and great laughs about my uniform. We became good friends and the next year I wore the proper uniform from Orvis and L.L. Bean.

Time passed and on November 30, 1967 (my birthday) I retired from Fusion-Rubbermaid, much to the chagrin of CEO, Don Noble, my boss. I had built five companies for Fusion, made mistakes at their expense, and also learned a great deal. It was time for me to go on my own—after all I was 40 and in my prime.

The spring of the following year I got a call from Frank indicating some interest in going in business together. We met in Statesville, and my first basic question to Frank was: "Why do you want to take the risk? After all only 1 in 10 ever succeed."

He replied very simply, "I want to be a millionaire."

I thought, "He is my man—he obviously has the right goals, ambition and selling skills." I did not ask any more questions. We would be on the look-out for a turn-around plastics business in the Toledo area, since Frank was established there, and I would stay in Statesville, NC and commute to Ohio as needed.

After months of looking at several companies, we reached the obvious conclusion: Why not start in the bottle business—especially since O-I had backed out of the PVC bottle business and Frank knew all the customers. Frank found we could buy the Bekum machines (4) that O-I turned down. Our good friend, Charles McKelvy, hunter and banker, offered us a million dollar loan if we could supply $200,000 of our own. That was possible, so we looked for a building to rent and found a large old government warehouse near Port Clinton. Another good friend, Greg Alexander, golfing buddy and lawyer, helped us form the company. As always, the problem was finding a name. After days of struggling, before dinner and after a few drinks, Frank, Susie and I settled on AIM Packaging—after an advertising agency I was involved in named AIM. Frank liked it because it put us at the top of the list in the telephone book and connected goals and ambition.

We were fortunate to get John Miller as the plant manager and Sam Carter as part-time (week-ends) accountant. Frank hit the road to get orders while John and I started setting the plant up. We put in the standard cost system used by Rubbermaid, accurately defining costs, and we were off and running by fall.

Frank and I found that we did indeed have a great deal in common. Our goals were #1 to succeed and #2 have fun doing it. Frank was the best salesman I had ever known (and I had hired plenty). He was magic with the customers. While I had experience in starting plants, running plants and knowing pricing and control of cost. We made a perfect team—complementing each other's abilities and the rest is history!

Years of expansion with high returns—we were soon millionaires and having the time of our life—golfing, hunting at our own lodge, fishing in the blue lake and 2nd homes on Marco Island. Our entertainment of customers with golfing everywhere, rental home on Hope Town, Abaco in the Bahamas. That was all great fun. Both families got along well socially and we enjoyed watching our children grow, fish and enjoy the sunshine.

John Miller, Sam Carter and Art McCamey brought a great deal to AIM Packaging and without their skills and help, we could not have profitably expanded. We owe a great deal to them.

Jim Caldwell who started the Wooster Rubber Company—Rubbermaid—always said "Business is people and they are most important."

I agree.

Appendix D

Letter from Samuel I. Carter, Executive VP
Administration, AIM Packaging, Inc.

When we first met at O-I Plastics, I was impressed by your dedication to "getting the job done" for O-I. Further questioning of others in the sales department confirmed your skills with customers. So when you asked me to come on board, I was comfortable with the decision to join your dream and help make it work.

Bob Ebert offered an opportunity to learn more about operations that was different form what I had experienced at Owens-Illinois and it permitted me to be a "sounding board" for John Miller when you were on the road selling. More late night calls than I care to remember.

Kathleen Harkness was the company "mother hen." She worried about everything and everyone, and most loved her for her thoughts and efforts. Gerry Behrn became the voice of AIM and was most effective with customers and suppliers.

Helene Curtis, Inc was a blessing to AIM, and a request from them was always honored if at all possible. The relationship you had built was a strong one. Few corporations would pay as promptly as they did—and on a couple of occasions wired funds not yet due to help a supplier cover a weekly payroll.

Nate Hoffman, Helene Curtis Director of Purchasing, was a character! Once when we had raised prices, he called in for you and you were out on sales calls. Gerry passed him to me. I listened for some period of time and then began to explain why the price increase was necessary now that we could continue to be a good supplier.

After quite a few minutes of discussion he abruptly asked "Whose nickel are we talking on?"

When I replied that he had called, his next question was about my name— Sam or Samuel? When I replied that it was Samuel but I prefer Sam, he then asked what my middle name was to which I replied, "Irvin."

He came back with "Samuel I understand. Irvin I can relate to. I don't know how Carter got in the act. You get your price increase." And promptly hung up. There after when we had a telephone conversation, one or the other usually said, "Whose nickel are we talking on?" and had a chuckle about it.

Another item: When we had customers at the lodge at Sand Beach, I would usually stock it with wine, beer and liquor based on who would be there. Jim Dalton, a purchasing agent, was the only one who never left anything behind—not even an empty bottle. Must have taken it with him as I checked the trash—not even one empty.

There are many memories of people and events that could go on and on. Bob, Art, Jim Foley who jumped out of the plane while taxiing down the runway approach when it backfired, and Russ Gervay who was a bit of a fish in the wrong pond with AIM, but an interesting person.

In closing, I wish to express the gratitude I feel for your having brought me in as a party to your dream and for letting me become a partner in it. It was a lot of hard work, but very rewarding in so many ways.

We do not see each other as often as we did at AIM, but the memories and concerns are still very much present. Enjoy good health, family, and whatever brings a smile to your face. Life is good my friend!

Appendix E

Letter from Arthur R. McCamey, Jr. Executive
VP Administration, AIM Packaging Inc.

Having had the opportunity to read and reflect upon the "Frank Harris Chronicles," I truly appreciate the invitation to comment on our strong friendship and those wonderful days at AIM Packaging. To those members of the Harris family, friends, business associates, and others given the opportunity to walk through you life, during the reading of your life story, they will discover a true Horatio Alger in their midst—truly an exciting and extraordinary story of a man on a mission.

Early in 1971, you and I had the opportunity to meet as arch rivals in the plastic bottle business. I remember the day you suggested that, "If you ever get tired of the big corporate life, let's talk about a future at AIM Packaging." Oh, that wonderful big corporate life that we all thought would lead us to fame and fortune, only to have that dream dimmed by a failure for the company to invest funds, as in your case, or the sale of the business to another company as in my case.

Starting to work at AIM the summer of 1972, my mission in life changed. It is hard to put in words the excitement I felt as you trained and mentored me during those early days at AIM. Bob Ebert and Sam Carter were also on hand to lend their guidance. You made business very simple compared to the large corporate secrets of hiding profitability.

I recall some of your famous statements;

Let's work hard and play hard.

When the customer says jump, we say how high.

Let's shoot all the birds, and sort them out on the ground.

Go to your supplier for research and engineering, it's too expensive otherwise.

I remember one of your more unusual business experiences involving our very largest customer. After having breakfast at the customer's home and you forcing me to eat more than my share of lox, bagels, and scrambled eggs, we joined him at his office. The critical part of the meeting was a price increase. We justified or you justified every cent of the increase, but after a long discussion and being reminded that our competition had not required an increase, the customer said, "No way."

If you recall, the customer fancied himself as a great putter, had a putter and miniature putting layout in his office. You said, "Why not putt for the increase." He smiled and reluctantly agreed. After all it was his layout. Much to his surprise you made three for three versus his two out of three. And we got the price increase. What a day!

You and I always shared the wonderful exhilaration when putting together a deal—large or small. In the early days it was the conversion of a major window cleaner from 40mm bottles to 50mm bottles and to plastic. As a result we supplied 100% of those bottles. That was a big deal, but could not compare to the deal that brought another customer's paid-for equipment to our plant, a five year commitment of loading machines and paying for the bottles as we accumulated a rail car or truck load in our warehouse. Any excess machine time could be used for alternate customer production. What deal!

While I touched on one of our strengths earlier, customer national rollouts of new products, I am sure no one appreciates our procedure of developing molds from approved drawings to production in four or five weeks. Our competitors were overrun by our ability to move so fast. We were in production before competition had an approved drawing.

We knew our employees on a first name basis, even some of their children. We met with every employee twice a year in very small groups and allowed them to "talk back to the boss." Probably one of the great reasons why we defeated the unions three times. I remember those all night sessions. We always discovered a procedure or process that could be improved.

On our personal side, we got to know each other's families. It was not a casual relationship. It was a strong relationship that came in handy when a crisis arose, and they did. We could depend on each other for advice and support.

One of our greatest testaments to our relationship is that after 18 years of working together and 19 more years of retirement, we are best friends and continue to have fun with each other on and off the golf course. Not many previous business partners can make that statement.

In closing, Frank, you and everyone that reads your biography should know how I feel about you. You were my most important mentor in my business success. I appreciate beyond these words everything we accomplished together. I am entirely grateful for all your assistance in making it happen for me.

Appendix F

A brief family history of Josh Rothman, former husband
of our daughter, Gingi, and father of our grandchildren,
Virginia Adair Rothman and Samuel Harris Rothman.
Thanks to Dusty Rothman for providing the following.

➺ Dorothy Lavon Leonard (Mother of Josh Rothman)

➺ Dorothy Lavon Leonard is the daughter of Maida Leolia Kesling and Richard Wilson Leonard. Maida was the only child of Dorothy McDaniel and Ballard Kesling. Dorothy McDaniel was the daughter of Melissa Bucy (who was born in Ireland) and Robert McDaniel (who was born in Scotland). Ballard was the son of Abraham Kesling who I think was born in Holland. Richard Wilson Leonard was the son of Arthur E. Leonard and Lavon Reese. He was their only child. When she died Arthur came home to be with his mother (whose maiden name was Bayley) to help her and have someone to help with his young son. He had a brother, Chick (Charles) who married a divorcee, Dorothy McDaniel Kesling, who with her young child, Maida, was living with her mother-in-law and her husband, Chick. The mother-in-law died and soon after Chick also died. Arthur and Dotty married the next year making Richard and Maida "brother and sister." They were about five years apart. When they were 18 and 23 they married. Five years later, in 1932, I was born. I was their only child. They divorced and in 1935 my mother married Arthur Ellis Daoust. His mother was Effie Herbster and his father was Stephen Daoust. I knew them as my grandparents as well as Dotty and Arthur Leonard. When we would go to the Leonard's home on Thanksgiving my biological father, Richard Leonard would be there with whichever wife he was married to at the time. He ultimately had five wives, all redheads whose names started with M. The atmosphere was always pleasant. Maida and Richard always seemed like brother and sister. Art Daoust was cordial to Dick Leonard.

➺ Fredric Burton Rothman (Father of Josh Rothman)

➺ Fredric Burton Rothman is the son of Samuel Rothman and Sophie Buck. Sam was born in Odessa, Russia, the son of Fanya Roitman. (The name was changed to Rothman when they arrived in the United States.) Sam had several sisters: Manya (Mary) who was a milliner who lived in New York. Emily who married Eugene Pinkus and immigrated to U.S. and moved to Toledo. And a brother Abram who spoke several languages and worked for the family of Aristotle Onassis. He lived in Istanbul and immigrated with his wife Fanya to the U.S. and lived in New York where he had several telephones. Depending on which one rang he would answer it in the language that it required. Samuel Rothman was sent to live with Abram in Istanbul because his mother found him carrying a gun for the Bolsheviks and shipped him off to live with his oldest brother. He came along with Abram and Fanya when they moved to the U.S. Sophie was born in New York, the daugher of Samuel Buck and Sarah Buck (who was born in Poland). Sophie had two brothers, Mac and David, and a sister, Sylvia (Sel). She met Sam in New York. They married and ultimately moved to Toldeo so Sam could work for his brother-in-law, Eugene Pinkus, in the steel business. Sam and Sophie had two more children after Fred: Stephen who is eight years younger than Fred and Lisa Jan who is eleven years younger than Steve, 19 years between Fred and Lisa. When I first went to Fred's house his mother came out to the car carrying this 18-month old child and when we pulled away from the driveway I said, "Whose child is that?" It looked like Fred. He said, "That's my baby sister." Whew!

Appendix G

A brief family history of Jennifer Kulczak Harris, wife of our son,
Walter, and mother of our grandchildren, Welles Francis Harris and
Grant Corlett Harris. Thanks to Jennifer for providing the following.

➤➤ Donald John Kulczak (Father of Jennifer Harris)

➤➤ Donald John Kulczak—born April 4, 1938 in Toledo, Ohio, the son of
Alphonse Kulczak and Janina T. (Bronowski) Kulczak. He married Janice
M. Easton. Attended Toledo Public Schools and enlisted in the Army
Reserves while still attending Woodward High School. Upon graduation he joined the Army where he became a Green Beret. After his time
in the Army, he continued in the Army Reserves for 15 years. He started
classes at the University of Toledo, but when Libbey-Owens-Ford (LOF)
offered him a job, they told him he wouldn't need to continue school,
so he started working full-time. He worked in the LOF offices 41 years,
mostly in the Payroll Department of Plant Accounting before retiring.

➤➤ Alphonse Kulczak—born 1913 in Toledo, Ohio. Died 1971 in Toledo,
Ohio. Son of Frank and Mary Kulczak. Married Janina T. Bronowski.
Enlisted in WWII in June of 1943. Worked for McManus Troup and
LOF.

➤➤ Frank Kulczak—born 1872 in Poland. Immigrated to U.S. in 1891. Married
Mary (?). Worked as an engineer on the railroad.

➤➤ Mary (?) Kulczak—born 1874 in Poland. Immigrated to U.S. in 1886.
Married Frank Kulczak.

➤➤ Janina T. (Bronowski) Kulczak—born in 1915 in Toledo, Ohio. Died
1961 in Toledo, Ohio. Daughter of Wincenty Bronowski and Katarzyna
(Sykowska) Bronowski. Married Alphonse Kulczak. She was a
housewife.

➤➤ Wincenty Bronowski (later Vincent Bronowski)—born April 20 1885 in
Russia where he worked as a Landmann. His father was Russian and his
mother was Polish. Married Katarzyna Sykowska. He departed Hamburg,
Germany to immigrate to U.S. April 2, 1910, arriving in Southampton,
NY. His ship to the U.S. was the President Lincoln. During Prohibition
was in "Liquor Distribution." Worked for LOF in the mix house.

➤➤ Katarzyna Sykowka (later Catharine (Sikorski) Bronowski)—born 1892
in Poland. Immigrated to U.S. in 1910. Married Wincenty Bronowski.

➤➤ Janice Marie Kulczak (Mother of Jennifer Harris)

➤➤ Janice Marie Kulczak—born January 22, 1944 in Toledo, Ohio. Daughter of Archibald M. Eaton and Florence M. (Furie) Eaton. Married Donald Kulczak. Grew up in Northwood and attended Lake Schools. Worked for LOF where she met Don. They married and moved to Perrysburg. Housewife for many years until daughters were older then returned to office work.

➤➤ Archibald Marion Eaton—born April 1, 1907 in Toledo, Ohio. Died May 1993. Son of John Ezella Eaton and Caroline A. (Hurdelbrink) Eaton. Married Florence Furie. As a young man he worked in a greenhouse for a florist. Later was a switchman for the Chesapeake and Ohio Railroad. Later worked in his father's commercial greenhouse.

➤➤ John Ezella Eaton—born 1880 in White Gate, Virginia. Son of Elbert Eaton and Ella (?) Eaton. Married Caroline Hurdelbring. He was a switchman for the Railroad and later owned a commercial greenhouse.

➤➤ Elbert Eaton—born 1841 in Virginia. Married Ella (?). Owned a farm. He served for the Confederacy in the Civil War, enlisteing July 15, 1861 at the Giles County Courthouse. His mother's name was Julia and his father was David Eaton Jr.

➤➤ David Eaton Jr.—born Sept. 7, 1820 in Virginia. Son of David Eaton Sr. and ? Married to Julia (?) Eaton. Owned a farm in Giles, VA. Died at the age of 39 after contracting pneumonia. Was sick only 10 days before his death, leaving his wife and 4 children—Elbert (1841), Milton (1845), Virginia (1850) and Marrieta (1857) to manage the farm.

➤➤ Julia (?) Eaton—born in 1818 and was married to David Eaton Jr. Lived in Giles, VA, was a housewife who later helped with family farm after her husband's death.

➤➤ David Eaton Sr.—born 1790 in Ireland. Immigrated to US and settled in Giles, VA.

➤➤ Ella (?) Eaton—born 1850 in Virginia. Married Elbert Eaton.

➤➤ Caroline A. (Hurdelbrink) Eaton—born 1881 in Woodville, Ohio. Her parents were both from Germany. Married John Eaton. She was a housewife.

➤➤ Florence Mary Fuire (DiFiore) Eaton—born October 4, 1911 in Toledo, Ohio. Died August 2001 in Perrysburg, Ohio. Daugher of Anthony

DiFiore and Teresa (Tesauro) Difiore. The first in her family to be born in the U.S. Married Archibald M. Eaton. She was a housewife.

↠ Anthony DiFiore (later Anthony Fuire)—born 1872 in Orria, Italy. Married Teresa Tesauro. This entertaining man owned a store and bar in Italy. He and his sweet, quiet bride lived above the bar. If she was upstairs and thought he was becoming too lively, she would stomp her high heel on the floor and he would know it was time to excuse himself and retire for the evening. He immigrated alone to the U.S. arriving at Ellis Island in 1907, while his wife and children waited until he was established in the U.S. He moved to Toledo where he worked in the shipyards and his family joined him a year later.

↠ Teresa (Tesauro) Difiore (Fuire)—born 1876 in Orria, Italy. Married Anthony DiFiore. Immigrated to the U.S. in 1908, bringing her two children with her (after losing two other children to a plague in Italy). Daughter Florence was their first child born in the U.S.